First
and Last Shots Fired
in
World War II

Marine Corps Memories
as told by Mack Abbott
to E. Wayne McDaniel

Library of Congress Catalog Number
2001095393

ISBN # 1-883793-44-0

Manufactured in the U.S.A. on archival paper

For additional copies of:
First and Last Shots Fired
in
World War II
Marine Corps Memories as told
by Mack Abbott
to E. Wayne McDaniel
Please mail $39.00
plus $5.00 shipping and handling to:
Mr. Mack Abbott
1968 Beechwood Blvd., S.W.
Gainesville, GA 30504
www.firstandlastshot.com

WOLFE PUBLISHING
P.O. Box 8036
Fernandina Beach, FL 32035
1-800-475-6782

DEDICATION

⊷⇒◉⇐⊶

    I want to dedicate this book as I dedicate my life; to my God, my Country, to the memory of Janie Abbott, my wife of 54 years, and my family.

\- Mack Abbott

My Family
Children

Carl Abbott	Pam Mock	Paul Abbott

Grandchildren

Russel Abbott	Brandi Bradshaw	Mallory Abbott
Kimberly Abbott	Shelley Mock	Nathan Abbott

Great grandchild
Christian Bradshaw

Mack Abbott and Great Grand-Child Christian Bradshaw

Table of Contents

Foreword

How does a lifetime full of memories, hand-sketched on a few steno pad pages grow into a book about a man's life and World War II? It takes endless hours of interviews, research and writing, then rewriting and rewriting again. Is it worth it? Resoundingly, yes!

For one thing, the process gave me the pleasure of getting to know on a very personal and intimate level one of the most interesting men I have ever met. Mack Abbott is a national treasure and the hundreds of conversations and phone calls we have had over the last couple of years has been an education and a glimpse back into a part of history that I missed only by a very few years. I accompanied Mack on many of his speaking trips and learned more about him each time because his talks are never twice the same.

I want to thank Kathy Dean, Mary Shephard and Betty Wolfe for spending myriad hours pouring over my manuscript and catching my many errors. I know they did not have the time to spare and I am grateful. Dan Jones, a Marine, and the Experimental Aircraft Association also gave of their time to help our effort. Thank you.

E. Wayne McDaniel

Remembering

It was just a few days before Memorial Day as I gratefully made my way to the old lawn chair and settled slowly into it. Working on the monument all morning had left me feeling a little tired and achy and bringing a chair from home had definitely been a good idea. The only other place to sit was on the stone benches near the monument but they were directly in the hot sunlight at this time of day. I had used up a lot of energy replacing eleven of the hundreds of blank-faced bricks in the monument's courtyard and I needed a little rest. Each new replacement was engraved with the name of a Georgia Pearl Harbor veteran who had passed away during the preceding year. The bricks made a perfect addition to the monument and it in turn added its beauty to the National Cemetery, but it was an awful lot of work putting down those new bricks every year.

My knees, often troublesome, now made their objections known as I slowly flexed and straightened them. I accept that a little pain is one of life's inconveniences and must be tolerated but I refuse to let it slow me down. At seventy-nine, I still have many plans and lots of important things left to do and I'm not about ready to give in to minor physical problems. I'm still quite vigorous and full of pep and can do a full day's work with the best of them. The knees do trouble me though, especially when I have to get down on the ground to work, whether on my azalea bushes at home or memorial bricks at the cemetery. Leaning back, I forced my legs out straight, pointed toward the memorial. A little rest in the coolness of this willowy shade tree seemed like a fine idea and I had earned a break.

I like shade trees, especially in the South where their sweet coolness is so pleasant and often necessary. Leaves rustled above me, dark green in the late morning sun as I thought for a moment about my old, spreading magnolia at home. They're my favorite shade tree and I particularly enjoy their creamy white blossoms. Maybe one would improve the setting here I thought, but then on second thought, I decided it wouldn't be a very good idea. They're so messy and shed nearly year round. The Cemetery staff is already kept plenty busy blowing leaves and other debris from the courtyard and they don't need more to contend with. The crew does an especially good job when preparing for our special ceremonies. Memorial Day weekend is the monument's busiest time followed by Pearl Harbor Day in December. The Sunday before Memorial Day brings many guests to the cemetery to pay their respects to Pearl Harbor veterans both living and dead.

A gentle breeze swept down across the thousands of graves that stretched away above me, then on downhill to the cemetery's front gate where an imposing arch guards the entrance. Most of the cemetery's original graves contain the remains of northern soldiers who died in Civil War battles fought near Atlanta and other engagements across the South. Northern officials ordered all fallen troops brought here and buried but local Southerners, who preferred calling the conflict "The War of Northern Aggression," found a separate burial site nearby for their war dead. Deceased veterans of more recent American wars have also been brought to the National Cemetery for burial nearly doubling its numbers to more than 17,000. A beautiful and peaceful burial ground, it provided us with the perfect spot to erect our memorial to Pearl Harbor veterans. There it sat before me now, a shrine to carve our names upon and preserve our memories for all time. As I leaned back and viewed the panoramic scene in front of me I felt a deep sense of contentment. Our beautiful monument, I thought, will make a lasting and fitting tribute to these veterans for countless years to come.

The monument belongs equally to every veteran who served at Pearl Harbor that long ago morning, those who died there as well as the ones who survived but have since passed on. My name will also be added here one day I thought, carved on my own memorial brick and placed by my son. When that day comes, nobody will remember that I had anything more to do with the project than any other veteran named here. That, I decided contentedly, is exactly as it should be.

All World War II veterans, living and dead, deserve recognition of course but I feel especially close to the survivors of that, *"Date That Shall Live in Infamy,"* as then-President Franklin Delano Roosevelt called the Pearl Harbor attack. December 7, 1941 is now many decades in the past but to those of us who were there many memories are still crystal clear and Pearl Harbor changed our lives forever. I receive calls nearly every day from survivors and their descendents who have only recently learned of the monument and want another brick of honor placed there. Our Survivors Association serves as focal point for the monument and I'm glad to be able to help with it, even in a small way. I also have an active interest in the two associations, the Survivors Association, as well as a newer one for their sons and daughters, which is quickly becoming a very special interest of mine. Both groups have a special attachment to our monument and that makes me feel remarkably good.

Each year as I replace several blank bricks in the courtyard with new ones engraved with the names and units of recently deceased veterans, I pause to reflect. There were eleven this year, a few more than last. Most survivors are past eighty now and it will soon fall upon their descendents to tell the Pearl Harbor story and uphold our message. I pray they will all help maintain the traditions and keep our country alert. Other sons and daughters organizations across the country already honor ancestors who fell in the Revolutionary and Civil Wars such as those buried here and in the Confederate Cemetery only a few minutes away. I want the Pearl Harbor story to be carried on in this same way.

Seventeen bricks in the front part of the monument's courtyard carry the names of Georgians who died at Pearl Harbor. They hold the place of honor and are easily identified by a distinctive color. Newer bricks for since-deceased veterans number one hundred and thirty with a few more added each year. There are several hundred plain bricks in the courtyard; some of them waiting to be replaced as newly engraved names join those of fallen comrades. I am honored to place the new bricks, answer questions about the monument and handle other association business. I was happy to be able to follow up on a friend's lead and help complete the project after he was unable to continue due to poor health.

My youngest son Paul has assured me that my work here will be carried on even after my brick is added. Every Georgia Pearl Harbor veteran's brick will have its place of honor and special days will continue to be observed. I'm proud to say that my grandchildren have also shown an interest in the project. As for me, I've chosen to devote the rest of my life to speaking about my experiences, helping promote both survivors' associations and proclaiming the message of Pearl Harbor. For many years after the war, however, I wouldn't even discuss the attack or its aftermath. I'm not sure why exactly but I just wouldn't talk about anything that happened over there and I still can't discuss many aspects of it.

Bringing the monument into being wasn't an easy task. Friend and fellow survivor, Ed Eads had originated the idea but soon after he enlisted my promise of support for the project and chaired the first committee meeting, he passed away. It was as if he had been waiting for me to sign on. The monument committee went on to raise more than twelve thousand dollars for the project, plus we also worked with cemetery officials who seemed intent upon placing the monument in a location other than its present ideal one.

Leaning back in the cool shade now I decided to rest a little longer before facing the Atlanta traffic on my trip back home to the foothills of North Georgia's mountains. As I relaxed, my thoughts drifted away, back some sixty years to that Pacific Sunday morning and I seemed to hear distant voices. One was my own while another person seemed to be addressing a group of people and I also heard a sound like many people murmuring softly in the background. Could I be dozing off and dreaming or was I hearing the buzzing of nearby insects? I'll rest a few more minutes, I decided, and then I really must head out, but it's so peaceful here in the shade and that humming sound is very soothing. I guess I may have dozed off about then.

"Good afternoon Ladies and Gentlemen. I'm your guide today as we tour the Marietta National Military Cemetery. We'll also be learning something about World War II in the Pacific and the new Pearl Harbor monument. Also, allow me to introduce Mr. Mack Abbott, a Marine who was at Pearl Harbor and later saw combat on many other islands throughout the Pacific."

"Marietta hosts two military cemeteries, both dating back to the Civil War. Here at the end of Cole Street sits the Marietta National Cemetery. The street was named in honor of Henry Greene Cole, a local citizen and Union sympathizer who donated the land we stand upon. Union operations against Atlanta followed by Sherman's March to the Sea and other campaigns left thousands of fallen soldiers buried in shallow, hastily marked graves all across Georgia and the need for a military cemetery near Atlanta quickly became obvious. Graves stretched from the northwest section of the state just below Chattanooga down to Atlanta, on eastward and over into the Carolinas. Clearly, something had to be done."

"Efforts by both sides resulted in two military cemeteries, one on the south side of Marietta, accommodating some 3,000 fallen Confederates and this one, which honors more than 10,000 Union war dead plus a very small number of Confederate soldiers. There are many more Union graves because often southern soldiers were taken home for burial. Several northern states have erected imposing monuments to their war dead in the National Cemetery. These memorials were placed soon after the Civil War ended but it is a new monument near the front gate that is of special interest today. This year's commemoration of the attack on Pearl Harbor makes our visit to honor this particular site especially meaningful."

"The first thing you see after passing through the arch is the handsome new courtyard and monument immediately on your left. It is dedicated to

Georgia's veterans of the surprise attack on Pearl Harbor December 7, 1941. Stone benches, roses and a dignified brick courtyard beckon you to enter and perhaps to pause once again before leaving. Hundreds of bricks are laid in front of a five-foot-tall slab of engraved marble, which sits on a two-foot pedestal. At first all bricks appear to be identical, but as you draw closer you notice that those nearest the entrance are a different color. Closer inspection reveals that one hundred and thirty bricks are engraved, each with a service member's name and military ship or unit. One color represents seventeen known Georgians who fell at Pearl Harbor on the morning of December 7th while others denote one hundred and thirteen veterans who have since passed away."

"One man who is in large part responsible for this monument is Gainesville resident Mack Abbott. As a young Marine, he was first out of his barracks to fire up at attacking Japanese bombers, torpedo planes and "Zero" fighters. Later, joined by about two dozen other Marines, he continued firing as aircraft swooped down to unload their deadly cargo and again as they returned to empty their machine guns, flying directly over his parade field. He fired as long as there were targets and stayed at his post until told to stand down."

"The newly promoted nineteen year old Marine Private First Class was up early for a Sunday morning, a traditional day of rest for many military personnel in Hawaii. Already dressed and breakfasted, he was spending a few minutes in conversation with buddies before leaving to take his first private flying lesson at the nearby civilian airport. There were many sorties flown that morning but he would not be among those getting into the air. Instead he remained on the ground, firing at as many enemy aircraft as he could bring his rifle to bear upon. Americans observe the anniversary of this event each year with ceremonies honoring Pearl Harbor veterans both living and deceased and December 2001, marked the 60th Anniversary of the assault with many special observances across the country."

"What was it like on that morning in 1941? Here is an abbreviated eyewitness account by a man who was up early to be ready for his exciting personal adventure. Waiting anxiously for his appointment time which was still a while off yet, he had no way of knowing the Japanese had a much more challenging experience planned, one that would last for the next several years. Could you please tell us about it, Mr. Abbott?"

I'd be happy to share a part of it with you. My buddies and I were taking it easy, sitting on my bunk near an open window to catch the breeze because the morning was quite warm. Suddenly, our conversation was interrupted by the sound of explosions coming from the harbor.

Contractors had been blasting down there earlier in the week but we thought it strange that they were working on a Sunday. Thinking instead that a naval exercise might be in progress, we went closer to the window to investigate. What we saw in the next instant satisfied us that this was no exercise. A two-seater Japanese bomber flew right by our window, so close I could almost have touched the wingtip. Every detail of the two men inside was plainly visible and if I had a rock I think I could have hit the plane. Since I was the only one dressed, I grabbed my gear and ran downstairs. I was the first man outside by several minutes. While my buddies, still dressed only in their "skivvies," rushed to throw on some clothes and grab weapons, I snatched my empty cartridge belt, steel WWI helmet, Model 1903 Springfield rifle, and charged outside. Rushing next door to the armory, I ran into a corporal who had his instructions and planned to follow them to the letter.

I asked for ammunition, but the corporal refused. "You got to have a requisition," he said. I was wondering what do to next when a sergeant rushed in, not very pleased with the corporal. "Break out that ammo now! The sky's full of enemy planes." I snatched a full bandoleer from the corporal, ran out onto the parade field and began firing while he and the sergeant began breaking open ammo cases. A few Marines from the barracks shortly joined me on the parade field bringing more ammunition and soon we were all busy firing at the enemy passing overhead. Of twenty-nine planes shot down that morning, Navy officials credited our little group with three official kills.

One of the planes we hit came down not far away, skidded across the grass, took out a tennis court and crashed into a family housing unit. A few of our men took a truck over there after the last wave of planes had departed, removed a wing and brought it back to the barracks. We all cut a little piece of the rising sun from it to help remember the day, as if we could ever forget it. I never forgot my experiences at Pearl Harbor or later on the Pacific islands of Palmyra, Midway, Guadalcanal, Tulagi, Saipan and Tinian. I kept my memories to myself, however, never discussing them with anybody, not even my wife Janie or my three children. Then, one Christmas several years ago, a special gift from my youngest son Paul broke my silence and I've been sharing many of my experiences ever since. I now tell my story to various groups, offering my personal philosophy on the war, the Marine Corps, and the future of our country. It took several decades before I began speaking about my experiences over there but now it's almost impossible to shut me up.

"It was about 15 years ago that I first became interested in my dad's wartime adventures," said Paul Abbott of Marietta Georgia. *"I asked my mother to show me his medals and she dug them all out for me. There were quite a lot of them and my wife Sherry and I framed them and presented them to Dad for Christmas. He was nearly overcome with emotion when his grandkids began asking him questions about the war and he began to tell us some of his adventures, although there are still some aspects he prefers not to discuss."*

I do talk more about it now, from Pearl Harbor right through the several years of fighting on the other islands. I also just happened to lead the last patrol on Tinian before the atomic bombs were dropped on Japan, ending the war. Saipan had fallen a few days earlier and I had attended that ceremony at the invitation of my C.O. who was stationed on Saipan but commanded all Marines on both islands. The enemy troops on Tinian evidently hadn't gotten the word because many were still holding out in caves and hiding in the cane fields. My C.O. at the time was Howard Kirgis, an officer I had also served under at Pearl Harbor. He later told me that I was surely the Marine who had fired the first and last shots of World War II and I guess I couldn't disagree with him, not that it really mattered much. I spent more than three months fighting on Saipan and Tinian before that last patrol. I was a sergeant and section leader by that time and had seen more than my share of combat.

One day a few years ago, fellow Pearl Harbor Survivor Ed Eads approached me. He said he had the dream of erecting a monument to Georgia's Pearl Harbor veterans, those who had died at Pearl and those who were later killed or passed away. He wanted me to help with the project and I said I'd be glad to do what I could. Tentative permission to put the monument inside the National Cemetery at Marietta was hung up awaiting a decision by the Department of Veteran Affairs, National Cemetery System about just where to locate it.

Not long after I signed on, Ed called asking me to come over to his house. *"Mack, I don't have long to live. I'm afraid I got you involved in this and now I'm not going to be around to help you finish it,"* he told me. A few days later, Ed Eads, Navy man, Pearl Harbor survivor, WWII veteran and one of the best boxers who ever fought in inter-service competition had lost his final bout to cancer. Ed had already designed the monument and set up a committee to start raising the money for it.

I left the monument just as Ed had originally intended it except for one or two minor changes. I liked the blue marble flag at the base, folded into a triangle as it would be after removing it from the casket at a military burial service, but something bothered me about it. There were five stars showing. Wasn't that too many for back then? It should display a triangular blue field and some stars, of course, but just how many? There were fewer stars on the flag in 1941 and I needed to find out the exact number visible when folded. I made calls to several cemeteries and veterans' groups but nobody could tell me until I got on the phone to Washington and finally got my answer. "Three stars would have been showing back in '41 sir," a government military historian advised me. That settled, all I had left to do was help the committee raise the rest of the money, iron out a few details with the cemetery folks, and we were in business.

Cemetery officials wanted us to put the monument way up on the hill next to the rotunda. After several discussions, I went up there and measured this way and that. Finally I told them I could only put it up there if permitted to cut down two or three trees that were in the way. I found out in a hurry that's one way to get cemetery people all riled up. They preferred to leave their trees right where they were and we finally agreed upon a location near the entrance.

The monument itself cost a little more than ten thousand dollars. A thousand more was needed for brickwork and another thousand for seeding and landscaping. An additional two thousand was put into a fund to ensure that no veteran will ever have to pay for his own memorial brick. Most of the money came from individuals giving twenty-five dollars or less but a few large companies donated as much as a thousand dollars. Veterans groups from around the state wanted to see the monument erected and gave what they could. Every cent helped and the committee and associations are very grateful to everyone who helped make the monument a reality. The result is a handsome memorial that enhances the National Cemetery grounds. Stone benches, rose bushes and the carving on the bricks all go to make it a favorite stopping site for visitors. Two vases sit on the pedestal, one at either end and during ceremonies one holds a red rose symbolizing those veterans still living and the other a white one to represent the deceased. Many visitors who have seen our memorial say they are moved by its simplicity and believe it to be one of the most beautiful they have ever seen.

There are memorials to two Medal of Honor recipients in the National Cemetery. One is Lee H. Phillips. His grave and marker are in Memorial Area B. The other is Sam S. Fuqua, who served on the battleship USS Arizona. A 41-year-old Navy Lieutenant Commander at the time, he was the senior survivor on the *Arizona* both in rank and longevity and is credited with saving numerous lives before the battleship sank and more after she went down. He is buried at Arlington National Cemetery but his memorial brick rests proudly among those in front of the monument. His daughter, Pat Nagle is a trustee for Chapter One of the Georgia Pearl Harbor Survivors Association and a member of the Sons and Daughters Association. She travels the country telling people of her father's heroic deeds that day. She was with her family overseas as a child, grew up in Asia and can tell many fascinating stories of her own.

Just a few bricks away from Sam Fuqua's, Ed Eads' name has been added to those of his comrades-in-arms. At 2 p.m. on the Sunday before Memorial Day, veterans, dignitaries and other interested persons gather at the cemetery's rotunda for a short ceremony. Then, led by a color guard, we slowly make our way downhill to the monument. Some veterans use walkers while others only need a supporting arm to make the short journey. A few take advantage of the spot where a portion of the curb has been removed to make the site wheelchair accessible. A closing prayer, leaving us with a sense of fulfillment follows a few more words at the memorial. Many folks linger after the ceremonies to reminisce about old battles and departed friends.

In December 2001, I flew to Hawaii for the 60th Anniversary observance of the attack. Thousands of veterans gathered to renew old acquaintances and pay homage to those that didn't make it. One topic of discussion was the movie "Pearl Harbor," which was released earlier in the year. There were a lot of mixed comments but most veterans liked the movie, even if they felt it was a bit fictionalized. Some felt the 30-year-old movie "Tora! Tora! Tora!" did a better job of showing the combat as it actually was but I liked both movies and thought they did a pretty good job of presenting what happened. I also like a good love story and the new movie includes an excellent one.

Many veterans attending the 60th Anniversary also made their way in small Navy boats across Pearl Harbor to Ford Island to visit a revered American memorial. They congregated above the *USS Arizona*, which still holds the remains of more than a thousand American servicemen who were trapped inside when she sank. For some of these war dead, monuments like ours in Marietta honoring Georgians who fought and died at Pearl Harbor provide their only stateside testimonial.

Every year, as I place more bricks for newly deceased Pearl Harbor veterans, I realize it will soon be up to our children and grandchildren to carry on for us. Mine are already showing an interest in helping me with the monument and keeping traditions alive. I also realize something else; unfortunately, freedom isn't free and vigilance is it's peacetime price, just as lives are sometimes the required cost in wartime.

I hold no real grudges against the Japanese people over the war. I believe they were caught up in a culture they were raised to believe in and had little control over. The fact that there were excesses can often be blamed on the culture and we have to get past that now. Many of my age group just can't make that adjustment and I understand their feelings, but I don't necessarily share them all. I respected the Japanese as soldiers and found them to be brave and their caves were always neat and clean. I hated the atrocities they committed, but I didn't hate the individuals. Some bad memories are still with me but I try to forget them whenever possible. History often turns former enemies into allies. It has happened in our own history a number of times and is still occurring today.

My story might not be the most important one around but I believe it definitely needs to be told. I've dedicated the rest of my life to sharing my experiences with as many people as possible, especially the younger ones. I plan to devote myself to promoting the ideals of "Remember Pearl Harbor" and the Survivors' associations as long as I'm able. That's the reason I give my talks and it's all the purpose of my book.

"Thank you Mr. Abbott. I'm sure I speak for all of us here when I tell you that I would like to hear as much about your life and exploits as you feel comfortable sharing with us."

I sank even more deeply into my comfortable chair. The breeze was gentle and smelled of freshly cut grass, a scent I've always liked. "OK," I said, "but I guess I'd better start all the way back at the beginning."

Growin' Up Rough

Many people who came into the world during my era grew up in very tough conditions. We were "Children of the Great Depression" and the living was far from easy. Hunger, lack of proper clothing, shelter and medical attention were all hard facts of our young lives. We did without toys or luxuries but more than that, we were often without enough to eat. The majority of us survived our childhoods but we never forgot the Depression and how very rough it was growing up back then.

I was born at Baptist Hospital in Birmingham, Alabama, 16 October 1922 and greeted my new surroundings kicking and screaming as most babies do. I would likely have made an even bigger commotion had I known how much shifting around from one place to another I would be forced to do all through my early growin'-up years. I didn't stay in one place very long as a child, and then I joined the Marine Corps and moved around some more. Mine might not have been the ideal childhood but it toughened me up and taught me a lot about life at an early age. The main difference between my earlier years and my time in the Corps was that I later moved from island to island rather than from household to household.

I also did a bit of kickin' against the bonds of authority during my childhood years. Had you known me then, you might have thought I was a bit of a troublemaker, but I never did anything really bad or dishonest, not back then or later on. It did take a lot of growin' up, however, to turn me into the kind-hearted, venerable gentleman I am now or at least try my best to be. Deep down I always had a fairly easygoing disposition but environment and circumstances sometimes worked together to bring out the worst in me. Times were terribly hard and sometimes you had to be tough just to get by.

I rambled practically from birth. I was always running somewhere I wasn't supposed to be and at the tender age of four or five I took my first great excursion by stowing away aboard a streetcar that stopped near our rented brick Birmingham home. I climbed aboard, hidden among the legs of adults and took off to explore the world. I enjoyed my long, free ride and stayed on until my crime was discovered when we reached the end of the line. Without any fanfare a very disturbed conductor put me off his car. He didn't ask when I had climbed aboard, where I lived or anything else, just deposited me on the sidewalk. I guess the poor man figured I had enjoyed enough free transportation for one day and wasn't about to give me a ride back home. I found myself all alone on the outskirts of Birmingham and near a big fairground. I went in and had a fine old time for the rest of the day, wanderin' around and seein' all the sights. I had no money but that didn't stop me from enjoying the constantly changing colorful scene. Also, I was small enough to wiggle into some really interesting places by again getting lost among the legs of grownups.

I guess I would have slept at the fairgrounds all night and continued my explorations the next day except for the nice lady that found me wandering around near closing time. She asked where I lived and then took me straight home. I must have really enjoyed that first roaming experience because, in spite of being punished, it wasn't too long before I decided to go ramblin' once again. When I was nearly six I jumped aboard a freight train that had halted just a few blocks from our house. The train soon rolled on and I was off on my next big adventure but unfortunately somebody spotted me. They pulled me off that beautiful, exciting train and carried me directly home to my parents again. That put a quick end to my second big adventure and I was really disappointed. I got punished pretty good that time and my visions of faraway places faded for a while, but I still liked to be on the move and would be again before long if at all possible.

I don't think my parents quite knew what to do with me during these formative years. I remember heart-to-heart talks, spankings and even being physically bound to my bed on several occasions. They had used up all conventional methods to keep me close to home and finally hatched a desperate but entertaining plan. One night not long after my aborted train ride, they decided to try frightening me into staying closer to home. I was lashed to my bed again wondering how to get loose and go exploring when I heard a noise right outside my window. Suddenly a ghostly specter rose up, an eerie light shining all around it. This took me by complete surprise and gave me quite a fright until when, after a minute or two, I figured it all out. It was my uncle, dressed up in his best Ku-Klux-Klan outfit and with a flashlight shining up into his hood and casting a ghostly glow. My father's brother made a couple of weird screeches for effect but when he heard me giggling he crept away in defeat. There was no doubt that I liked to ramble but I was soon going to get more of it than I could have hoped for.

My parents enjoyed socializing with friends back then and some of my earliest childhood recollections are of their parties. There was some drinking going on, but not too much I guess. My father did sometimes make his own home brew and I usually was called upon to help him. After he brewed and bottled his concoction, my job was to cap it off. Manufactured liquor, except for dangerous bootleg booze was just about impossible to come by in those Prohibition days, so many people simply made their own.

In January 1920, two years before I was born, Congress passed the Eighteenth Amendment to the Constitution. It prohibited all manufacture or sale of alcoholic beverages and was probably the most hard-fought and controversial law ever enacted in our history. Most folks, it seemed, just didn't like other people telling them what they could or couldn't do or drink and home brewing of beer and strong spirits was one way to get around the Prohibition laws.

My parents did have their fair share of domestic problems and my mother could be a little headstrong and overbearing at times. I have some distant memories of their arguments but my dad was always very easy-going and patient and this usually quieted things down on the home front. When I was seven, my parents separated and later divorced, something quite unusual in those days. My mother left town headed for parts unknown and we later heard she had been up to Tennessee and then down to Atlanta. My father moved into a room at the old Morris Hotel on First Avenue in downtown Birmingham. The room was quite small and he was at work most of the time, so it was decided I should move across town and live with my Aunt Sarah and her family and come visit him on occasional weekends. This began my real travels, which would soon give me more ramblin' than I had bargained for.

My mother's sister Sarah lived in the Fountain Heights section of Birmingham and my maternal grandparents lived not too far away. I looked forward to being closer to them and closer to my cousins, too. Sarah had two boys, Ray who was about my age and Frank, a couple of years older. We had some good times while I was staying with them and Ray and I really had more than our fair share of fun together. I soon found out he was a "rambler" too.

There was always plenty to eat at Aunt Sarah's but she wasn't very big on variety. This was especially true at lunchtime when she was usually busy washing and cleaning. The school grounds came right up against our back yard and I remember running home with the boys for lunch every day, a meal that never varied. We rushed in hungry and there on the kitchen table stood our three sandwiches and big glasses of milk. The sandwiches never varied, always peanut butter and bananas between two generous slices of white bread. Our lunch was filling and tasted good so we never complained because we knew many people weren't getting enough to eat and would be glad to have our peanut butter sandwiches.

I didn't have many chores to do at Aunt Sarah's but I did get assigned the job of chief cigarette maker for my uncle. He was a heavy smoker and rolled his own, or rather had me roll them for him. I sort of enjoyed the job because I didn't have to do it by hand. He had an old Target Tobacco cigarette-making machine that did all the work for me. All I had to do was shake the right amount of tobacco onto a cigarette paper, which I had moistened along one edge and placed on the little platform. One push on the handle, the thing flipped over and out popped a perfect smoke. I never tried one of them for myself although I had plenty of opportunities.

My cousin Ray and I soon devised a method to cover even more distance in our travels around town. We scrounged up an old pair of roller skates somewhere, found a few scrap boards and made ourselves a fine scooter apiece, sort of like the ones so popular with young people today. Of course, ours were very rough looking because we were too poor to afford the proper materials, but they worked great. With our scooters, Ray and I really covered a lot of territory. I guess we must have gotten into quite a lot of mischief as well because before long Aunt Sarah decided that I had to go. My next stop was to be a Catholic boarding home and school.

All the boys at my new home shared one big open room with beds all lined up in rows. Mine was an old iron model and not very comfortable as I remember. We each had small wooden chests in which to keep our meager possessions and that was about it. There were more than twenty-five boys in that vast room. Way down at the end of the open bay was a small chamber reserved for the sister who served as our night monitor. I never knew why I was sent to a Catholic school because my parents were Methodists. My time at this school was short but it was filled with great learning experiences, which I was lucky to acquire at such an early age. The sisters did a good job of teaching discipline and caring for us.

On Sundays the nuns assigned me a special job that I enjoyed and felt quite proud to have. I was to light all the candles before every mass and put them out afterward. I did a really good job with those candles and the sisters seemed proud of me too. I didn't do nearly so well at schoolwork in spite of the sisters' efforts with the end result that I failed the third grade. I don't know why I often did so poorly in school in my early days. The work wasn't that hard for me and I had little trouble with academics in later life. I think I just must have had too many other things going on in my mind distracting me.

With summer, came vacations and all the other boys left to spend time with their families. My parents being split up, I didn't really have a home to go to so I remained at the boarding school all alone, save for the nuns. I stayed in that big dormitory room all by myself each night, except for the solitary sister asleep in her tiny cell way down at the end. It was lonesome with only those lined-up empty beds and the distant nun for company. It was depressing as well as lonely but I managed to get by. On warm summer days I helped the sisters work in their flowerbeds and garden and I liked that a lot. They gave me another special task that I enjoyed almost as much as lighting the candles. My new job was to take an old wheelbarrow to a nearby pasture and shovel up every nice, dry cow chip I could find. We then used them to fertilize the garden and flowerbeds. It was great to be off by myself for a while exploring the pasture and nearby woods.

Some weekends I visited my father at the hotel and occasionally he gave me a quarter for a Saturday movie matinee. For five cents I could see a double feature, cartoon and the news. I usually bought myself some candy and after the show hurried to a nearby hotdog stand to purchase a giant dog with sauerkraut and onions, also a nickel. Then I used my last few cents for the streetcar ride all the way back to the Catholic school.

With the end of summer, my stay at the school was also over. I left there and moved on without ever really knowing why, this time to live with a farm family near a little rural town not far from Selma. I think the Catholic school may have been proving too expensive. The Great Depression put many youngsters to work on farms for just room and board and most considered themselves lucky to have a bite to eat and a roof over their head at night. I lived on that farm for two years and worked hard all the time I was there. I was still just a youngster of nine or ten but everybody on the farm had to "pull their weight."

One of my jobs was to milk the old, sway-backed cow every day so there would be a little fresh milk for the table. It was obvious from the first moment that the cow didn't like me. Our relationship was uneasy at best and at other times became a real war of wills. The farmer first showed me how to wash "the bag," as he called it. He then taught me to work the milk down from the top of each teat to the tip, then strip out every last drop of milk and he also used another word for teat that shocked me the first time I heard it. He soon left me to finish the job while he went off to his other chores. I sat down and grabbed a double handful of cow, and she promptly whacked me severely on the side of the head with her tail. It hurt like the dickens but that wasn't the worst part. She had recently coated her tail with a fresh batch of slimy, smelly manure apparently in joyful anticipation of laying it up beside my ear. I gave that old cow a tremendous poke in one of her several stomachs and prepared to get on with the job. Cow thought things over for a while, biding her time until my bucket was nearly filled with fresh, frothy milk, then she delivered a mighty kick ninety degrees sideways that sent me sprawling into the corner, the now-empty bucket in my lap.

As the barn cat hungrily slurped up this unexpected bounty, I went down to the end stall, found an old two-by-four, carried it back and sat it down near Bossy's head. She eyed it with suspicion as if she might have already met it a time or two and went rigid as a statue. I finished the milking without any more trouble and took my partially filled bucket into the house. The farmer's wife peered unhappily into the milk pail. *"Didn't give much did she?"* she complained. *"Are you sure you got it all?"* I figured enough time had gone by for the cat to have lapped up all the evidence, so I said, "Every drop. You can go check for yourself and I think you should give that stingy old cow a good beating while you're at it." Eventually the cow and I gained a grudging acceptance of each other. I never failed to tie her nasty tail to the stall side with binder's twine before I sat down to milk and I guess she figured another kick would just bring out the two-by-four again. We got along passably well from then on but never did become what you would call good friends.

Nearly everything we ate came from the farm and there was usually enough of something or other to go around but I had to work hard for my supper. I had lots of other jobs around the house and old barn, cleaning up, feeding animals, pumping buckets full of fresh water and working in the garden. My time on that farm was far from a vacation. Their philosophy was that I was put there to earn my keep, such as it was, and they did their best to make sure I did my fair share day in and out.

In the middle of the little town stood an old wooden water tank. It's shaky supports were probably eighty feet tall. To a boy my size it looked taller than Jack's beanstalk and was just begging to be climbed. I couldn't resist a challenge like that for long so one late summer afternoon I took off to town planning to scale the thing. There was an old, rickety ladder that pulled down until it almost touched the ground. I jumped up, caught hold and away I went. It was a long way to the top but I just kept looking up and climbing, step-by-rickety-step. After what seemed like a long time I found myself standing inside the railing that ran around the tank. I was up so high I could see for miles. Soon however, I remembered my need to get down and back to the farm chores before I was missed, but I had failed to notice one important thing on my way up. For the last few feet at the top the ladder angled out to the edge of the tank. When it came time to hook my feet into that old, shaky ladder and climb down, it seemed to just fall away into open space and I froze like a cat up a tree. I stayed up there until dread of being discovered outweighed any fear of the possible death awaiting me below. I finally just wrapped my legs around the ladder, hugged it tight, climbed down and went back to the farm. They had missed me by this time and I got into quite a bit of trouble. When I left the farm after two years and moved back to Birmingham, I landed in what today would be called an "abusive" situation. Back then there were no agencies to help with that sort of problem and you either endured it or sorted things out for yourself.

I'm not sure if my leaving had anything to do with the water tower incident because I was never told what was going on back then. I wasn't too crazy about farm life, but had I known what was waiting for me at the next place, I would have tried my best to stay on right where I was. I went back to Birmingham to board with a family I had never met before. They had a son who was quite a lot older than me and half-again my size, and John was not very pleased to make my acquaintance. He soon took great delight in pushing me around and trying his best to make my young life as miserable as possible. He didn't like having me horn in on his family life and share his dinner table and so on, but he especially hated me at bedtime. We had to share the same bed because there just wasn't any other place for me to sleep and John never missed an opportunity to make it painfully plain to me just how little he enjoyed that. I'm sure his mother took me in for the extra few dollars it brought her, as any additional income was very welcome back then. Many people didn't have a bed at all, so I guess I was still pretty lucky but I paid for my keep by taking abuse from John, who was just a big bully, but I soon decided I wasn't going to take it forever.

I was still having problems at school and could never seem to get my homework done what with John constantly picking on me and all the other distractions. I quite often found myself in a room at school that I didn't have to share with anyone. The coatroom became my own private haven because the teacher stuck me in there nearly every day to punish me for some minor infraction, imagined or otherwise. That coatroom became my little home away from home, if you could even call John's place a home. I also spent my share of time in the book room, waiting for a visit from the principal. The book room held extra textbooks and also served as a punishment room for boys the teacher sent "to the office." I remember the principal as a big man with hairy arms who seemed to enjoy working little boys over with his big wooden paddle. It had holes drilled in it intended to make each whack hurt even more. It was a very efficient design as most schoolboys of my era can testify and it hurt like the dickens. It soon got to the point where I played hooky and rambled more often than I went to school, preferring the fields and woods to either John's house or the school. I had always liked best being on my own anyway.

I didn't have much to call my own back then except an old switchblade knife that I had traded for and in the end it solved my problems with John. It was quite long and nasty looking and the "click" sound it made when it snapped open gave me some small feeling of security. One day when I had finally taken all of John and his attacks I could stand, I took out the knife, clicked it open and cut him a little bit with it. I didn't wound him badly, just enough to make him stop hurting me and it worked out even better than I expected. I couldn't think of anything else to do, him being so much older and bigger than I was. I had taken it for as long as possible, but now here he stood, bleeding and hollering about how he was finally rid of me. He looked pretty silly at that moment but I didn't dare laugh because he might have killed me although he kept his distance from me until I left. They called my father and he eventually came and picked me up. It was none too soon for me and I was happy when he informed me that I was coming home to live with him and his brand new family.

He had recently remarried and I went to live with him, his new wife Clara and her daughter Adriane. They all lived out at the foot of Red Mountain on the outskirts of Birmingham but I would have gone anywhere to be back with my father and away from John. I missed my mother of course but we hadn't heard from her and didn't even know where she was. There wasn't much I could do about that until one day when my father greeted me with some tremendous news. *"I got a letter from your mother,"* he announced. *"She's married and living in Jacksonville, Florida and she wants you to come down there for a few weeks during summer vacation."* I didn't really know what to make of this event but I did know I wanted to see my mother and if at all possible I would go down to Florida and visit her. As soon as summer came and school was out, my father took me to the Greyhound station and put me on a bus for Jacksonville. It was a long, uneventful ride taking all day to get there.

I hadn't seen much of my father during these years but I hadn't seen my mother at all. I had visited him at his hotel a few times but this was my first chance to see her and I was looking forward to it. She and her new husband Clarence picked me up at the Jacksonville bus station. I was really glad to see her but I decided right away that I didn't care too much for Clarence and I guess that's probably natural in a situation like that. I met Clarence's mother, Mrs. Flynn and liked her right away. She worked in a department store and I didn't know it then but I would meet her again at a later date and she would save me from near starvation.

There wasn't much for me to do in Jacksonville. We went to the beach several times but the jellyfish were so thick in the Atlantic that summer they took all the fun out of swimming. I got stung a couple of times and that put an end to our beach trips. One day I discovered a big pile of what looked like scrap lumber in the garage and found a tree nearby that looked like it would be a great place for a tree house. I asked Clarence about the lumber and he told me I could have it and promised to pick up some nails for me the next day. I spent the rest of my vacation days building myself a tree house. It turned out to be a really good one but about the time I finished it just like I wanted, I found myself on the Greyhound once more and headed back to Alabama.

My first Christmas back with my father I received a very useful gift, a second-hand bicycle. On Saturdays I used it to deliver orders for a little local grocery store. On weekdays I went door-to-door selling "Liberty Magazine" for a nickel. I made some pocket money this way and even managed to save a little. I also kept the lawn mowed and helped Clara in her flower gardens. In winter, I banked up the fire in our furnace every night and got up real early next morning to get a nice fire burning before anyone else got up. I also made myself a chinning bar out of some old two-by-fours and a short length of scrap 3/4" steel pipe. I put it up in the back yard and did chin-ups every chance I got. The work on the bar built me up in a hurry and soon I was doing some acrobatic tricks on it. Time passed quickly and I was soon twelve years old and in the 7th grade but I still wasn't doing especially well in school. Clara tried to help me and through her efforts I had a little more success with "the three Rs." She was also very strict on manners around the house and I learned some more discipline from her.

Like many men of his era my father didn't drive a car. On Sundays we would all get into a cab for the ride to church. Clara had been attending this church for a long time and soon we were all going regularly, a habit I still stick to. My stepsister Adriane and I were about the same age and she was very good at schoolwork. She set a good example for me and I began doing even a little better at school. She took dancing lessons all the time as well but I wasn't about to go that far just to fit in. I really liked Clara and Adriane and we became good friends, getting along fine together. I don't know what became of them later on and I just lost track of them in the turmoil of the years that followed.

At school I made a friend who had a special talent and big dreams. Jeff longed to become a champion boxer and often used me as his sparring partner when polishing up for his weekend bouts. He was also older and bigger than I was but I had grown some too and sometimes got lucky and gave back nearly as much as I took from him. He fought nearly every Saturday night and got paid five dollars when he won a match. If he lost he only got two bucks and this never failed to make him angry. The week's sparring was always a lot rougher following one of Jeff's losses and I then often served more as a punching bag than a sparring partner.

I still spent much of my time alone during those days and often climbed up on Red Mountain to be all by myself. The mountain was laced with old abandoned iron ore mines and I enjoyed exploring deep into the shafts looking for whatever I could find. I liked it high up on that mountain with no houses or people around because it was peaceful and I spent hours on end without interruption. My father had served in the Army in the Great War, later called World War I and had brought home a souvenir German bayonet. I took that big old bayonet with me whenever I climbed the mountain and had a grand time using it to chop and dig. I found a lot of little sassafras trees up there and often dug up a few. I cut off the roots, took them home, cleaned them and we boiled up a great big pot of sassafras tea. Everybody enjoyed that because sassafras tea was popular when I was young. People used to drink it often and considered it a healthy tonic although there's some argument about that now. I still have that old bayonet and I treasure it to this day.

I later started taking a new friend up on the mountain with me. Bill lived nearby and we went to school together. It soon became our regular routine to hike up the mountain looking for adventure. We found more mine shafts and gave several their own special names. Soapstone had walls full of loose soapstone and we spent many hours carving animals and toys from the soft material. One was always ice-cold no matter how hot the day so it became Refrigerator Shaft. Many had rails which ran between them, then around and on down the mountain. One day Bill and I discovered an old abandoned ore car, pushed it up as high as we could, then jumped in. It was quite a ride and we stayed with it until it finally stopped. It then became our habit to push that old car up on our way to the shafts. It wasn't too difficult because the track wound around the mountain several times. When we were ready to go home, we jumped in and rode down as far as she would carry us. I still treasured my privacy and sometimes went up on the mountain alone. My favorite pastime then was to stretch out flat on some grassy hilltop and daydream, mostly about the unusual life I had experienced so far. I didn't know it but things weren't going to become very routine for many years to come.

An artist lived next door named Mrs. Kay and she paid me a quarter once or twice a week to sit for her paintings. It was always the same pose, me wearing shorts but no shirt with my bayonet strapped to my side. I could always use a little extra spending money so I didn't mind too much and Mrs. Kay seemed well satisfied with her paintings.

About the time I finished 8th grade, I heard my mother was back in Atlanta. Aunt Sarah received a letter from her that included a return address. I wrote down the address, took it to my father and told him I wanted to go try and find her. I thought he would say no but instead he simply gave me two dollars with his blessing and I set off hitchhiking to Georgia. He didn't say much when I left but I got the impression he felt I should go locate my mother if at all possible.

These days you can drive from Birmingham to Atlanta in a few hours but my trip took three long days and nights. The first night I slept in a little park but the next two found me stuck way out in the country. No problem, I told myself, I'll just camp out on the ground. I curled up in the woods at the side of the road and slept like a log. The trip was quite an adventure and I really enjoyed being by myself, making do with whatever was at hand. Most of my rides were quite short, usually from one rural town to the next in the back of a farmer's pickup truck and I also walked a good part of the way.

When I got to Atlanta I learned from neighbors that my mother had left Clarence and gone back to Florida. Both of them had disappeared and no one knew where. It was too late to turn back so I headed for Jacksonville, figuring she must have returned there. When I reached the city I couldn't find her so I looked up the only other person in town I knew, Clarence's mother. Luckily, I remembered how to find the store where Mrs. Flynn worked. I had fond memories of this lady from when I had visited Jacksonville before. She was a kindly woman and seemed genuinely glad to see me. After taking one look at me, Mrs. Flynn told her boss she was taking lunch and away we went to a restaurant where she bought me a great big meal. I must have looked half-starved because she rummaged in her purse and gave me another two dollars to help me on my way. She then told me that since Clarence and my mother had split up a few months earlier she had no idea where either of them had disappeared to but had heard a rumor that my mother had gone to Miami. I thanked her and hit the road once more, this time headed due south.

I recalled that my mother had two good friends living in Miami, a Mrs. Standford and a Mrs. McWhirter. I couldn't think of a better plan, so I spent the next several days hitchhiking down the Florida coast. I arrived in Miami late on a Saturday night, looked in a phone book and found the Standford's address. I decided to try there first and asked a passing man how to reach the street. That night I located the house but it was quite late and all the lights were already out so I entered a nearby park and bedded down for the night. Bright and early next morning I went to a nearby filling station, washed up and tried to make myself a little more presentable. All those nights on the road, sleeping on the ground in the same clothes and missing meals had really taken their toll on my appearance but I bravely went right up and knocked on the door. My mother answered, grabbed me and gave her just-turned-thirteen son a big hug. I was glad because I didn't know what I would have done next had I not found her. She was surprised and glad to see me but shocked at my appearance. I must have looked pretty scruffy and as hungry as I felt because she sat me down and gave me a huge, delicious breakfast. I was feeling great again in no time.

We stayed with the Standfords for a few days and I was just beginning to get settled when my mother told me we needed to talk and took me for a walk. She told me Clarence had contacted her again. She didn't say how he had found her but he was back in Atlanta and she had agreed to go back with him. Thinking it over later I decided she must have contacted him first but either way we were soon headed back to Atlanta. Boy, I thought, I could have saved myself a lot of wasted miles and missed meals had I only known all this earlier but I didn't say anything since I was quite used to living with uncertainty by this time. When we got back to Atlanta we moved into Clarence's small room in a boarding house and I didn't like the living conditions there at all. Here I was, thirteen, almost a man and I had to share a room with my mother and Clarence, a man I didn't care for all that much anyway. I had a cot curtained off in the corner where I slept but there was very little privacy for any of us. The bathroom was down the hall and we had to share it with several working men.

The lady that owned the boarding house was a great cook and this helped cheer me up some. All the boarders ate together at one time, sitting around a big table passing along huge platters of food. The landlady really knew how to satisfy a hungry crowd's appetite. One day we had corned beef and cabbage, the next chicken and dumplings, then a hearty Irish stew and so on until the weekend. We ate light on Saturdays but Sunday was reserved for Georgia-style Southern Fried Chicken with green peas, mashed potatoes and gravy, half-runner pole beans, corn bread, biscuits and sweet tea followed by a big slice of pecan or apple pie. It was good eating and I quickly regained the weight I had lost on my road trips.

I soon found a job selling door-to-door, discovered a natural talent and did very well at it. I offered customers a club plan where they joined to receive discounts on such well-known magazines as *Better Homes and Gardens, Cosmopolitan* and *Redbook*. This was the first time I had ever earned any real money of my own and soon I was making enough to save quite a bit each week. Every payday they announced who had sold the most and I was often named their number one salesman. When summer was over I started back to school but continued to sell my magazine plan on Saturdays. I was doing pretty well in school now and Saturday sales still brought in some extra money.

One Sunday in October, my mother and I were sitting on the front porch enjoying the fresh air while Clarence leaned against the railing. He was a big man and suddenly the rails gave way with a loud crack.

Clarence went over the side and landed flat on his back with a tremendous thud six feet below. The porch boasted five perfectly good steps but he had discovered a much quicker way down. There he was, in the middle of a flower patch groanin' and carryin' on like he was about to die. They rushed him straight to a hospital where it turned out he wasn't seriously hurt, just had the wind knocked out of him plus a few bruises and scrapes. Clarence came out of his ordeal a relatively rich man for those times. The boarding house lady's lawyer quickly offered him $500 not to sue for damages. It was a princely sum in those days and Clarence promptly grabbed it.

A couple of days later my mother and Clarence had the bright idea to take the $500 and move down to Orlando. Clarence bought an old car, I pulled out of school again, and we all piled in with what little we owned, and took off. We drove to Florida and rented a small house. About the only thing I enjoyed about this next period was that Clarence would sometimes let me drive his car to the store or on short errands all by myself. He was a little on the lazy side so he gave me a few quick driving pointers and off I went, thirteen years old, behind the wheel with no driver's license and feeling on top of the world, if even for a short time.

Clarence eventually found work as a salesman with a big plumbing company. I applied at the same place and they hired me to work in their shop building solar water heaters. These heaters worked very effectively in the hot Florida sunshine. We first fabricated a shallow tank about three inches deep, a three-foot by six-foot oblong made of aluminum sheets, which we had painted black to absorb the sun's rays, then covered with a heavy glass top. Three-quarter inch copper pipe connected the device to a second tank holding thirty gallons of water. After we assembled the heaters in the shop, a team took them out to install. I often went along to help with this part of the job too. I liked the work and happily took to engineering water systems later on in the Marine Corps and then in later life.

At the end of summer, I started back to school but I was soon to be on the move again. About half way through the year, my mother left Clarence yet again and we moved into a little one-bedroom house in back of the landlord's larger home. Our new place had a small kitchen and bath and was nice enough but I quickly got the impression we were hiding out. Another big problem was that the water hadn't been turned on yet and the landlord told us it might take a week or more to get it going. I don't know what they expected us to do in the meantime, but I came up with my own solution. I was pretty resourceful even back then and each night after everyone was asleep I slipped up to the big house and quietly turned on the outside faucet. Undetected, I filled pans with water and carried them home. I made several trips each night and kept us supplied with plenty of water to drink, cook with, do the dishes and flush the toilet. In a little while we left this house and moved in with a lady my mother had met in town and rented a room from. Clarence didn't know where we were but he was probably looking for us and pretty sore. I learned my mother had taken half of the money remaining from his accident and I don't think she told him anything about it. I'm sure she felt entitled to it but Clarence probably would have disagreed and like I said, he was a big man.

Soon my mother and I had another talk during which I learned of her plans to return to Miami and find work. I think she figured finding a town that Clarence wasn't in was also a priority. Not only was he a husky man but he wasn't easy-going like my father. I was to stay in Orlando and lay low until sent for, she told me, hopefully soon. In a short while I received a letter with a bus ticket and instructions for me to join her in Miami. She had rented a room from a Mrs. Mosely, the mother of an old friend from Birmingham, who now lived in Miami, named Mrs. McWhirter. We now lived near each other in the Coconut Grove area of Miami and her son Jim, who was about my age and I soon became great friends. I would have to say he was the best friend I had while growing up and I was happy recently to discover he now lives near me in Northeast Georgia.

Shortly after we moved into Mrs. Mosley's house, I started back to school in the ninth grade. It was very hard, always falling back and starting over and besides I really needed to work full time to help my mother make ends meet. Times were still plenty tough so after just a couple of months I quit school. I needed some type of ride to reach a job from Coconut Grove, so I took the little stash of money I had saved, borrowed a bit more from my mother and bought a motor bike. It was a little one-cylinder job you had to push to get started. Once going though, it rolled right along and took me wherever I needed to go. It was a real lifesaver.

As soon as I got the motorbike, I began scanning want ads for a job and soon found a listing asking for a truck driver. Since I had driven Clarence's car several times I felt pretty competent behind the wheel. I can do this job I thought, so I applied and got hired the same day. I was to be a delivery driver for a food supply company but first the owner told me I needed a truck driver's license, and off he sent me to the local police station to get one. I was nervous, but in no time I had my commercial driver's license. I always wondered if my new employer had put in a good word for me with the police because I had just turned fourteen years old.

My job started every morning at 5:30 a.m. sharp and after I loaded my truck I took off on my rounds in the city. My new employer was the Rutherford Food Products Co. in Coral Gables. They sold large containers of olives, cherries and other food products including gallon-sized jars of fruit juice and salad dressing to bars, restaurants and schools all over Miami. After making my deliveries I brought the truck back and serviced it for the next day. I usually got finished around four o'clock, then jumped on my motorbike and headed for home. I enjoyed the job and the extra money really helped out too. The Rutherford family was very good to me and treated me more like a son than an employee. I was starting to feel pretty good about things in general and especially enjoyed learning the neighborhoods of Miami and the surrounding area where there was always something interesting to see. The pay was quite low but I was grateful for any work and I grew more thankful for my little motorbike every day. It was loads of fun and a whole lot better than walking or riding a bus to work. The time I saved meant I could sleep a little longer in the mornings and when you start at 5:30 that's a big plus.

My mother's friend, Mrs. McWhirter let her son Jim borrow the car some weekends and we went riding. Several years had passed, Jim and I had grown some and it was about this time that I discovered girls and we began double-dating. I also bought a little .22 rifle and on nights when we didn't have dates, Jim and I would drive out onto the Everglades highway and practice shooting. I also made a trip to a tattoo parlor with a couple of friends one day and had the man put an eagle and American flag on my arm. I don't think my mother cared for my new tattoo but she didn't say too much. I had turned seventeen by then and I guess she thought I was man enough to make my own decisions.

I had a new job working with Jim at Dade Pharmacy for better pay. Jim's uncle had recommended him and they both helped me apply and the extra money was a very welcome addition at home. Our job was to uncrate drugstore items and stock the shelves. After that we filled our orders and made deliveries all around town.

At seventeen all males were required to register for the draft. When a boy turned eighteen, if he wasn't in school, there was a good chance he would be drafted into the Army. I asked my mother if she would sign giving her permission for me to go into the Marines at seventeen and she agreed. The war in Europe was in full swing by this time and even though the U.S. was staying out of it for the time being, attitudes were rapidly changing about isolationism. Excesses by Germany and Italy in Europe and by Japan in China were stirring up American blood. More and more people were muttering that we should do something more to help out before the United States was attacked. Recruiting posters were everywhere and people said we would probably be at war soon, if not with Hitler then with the Japanese. The Marines up on those recruiting posters looked so fine I could hardly wait to become one. I went to see the Marine recruiter and he sent me for a physical, a requirement before enlistment. After the examination the doctor told me I had a couple of varicose veins that would have to be taken care of before I could enlist. Nothing major, he told me but I would have to rest for six months after the operation. Then he set up the surgery at a charity hospital so I wouldn't have to pay. I went in right away and had my operation. Now I faced a long six-month wait.

In the meantime, my mother and I still needed my income so I found a temporary job as a bellhop at the Cadillac Hotel on Miami Beach. The work wasn't too heavy because there were handcarts for the luggage and I made some good tips, especially if someone had a good day at the racetrack. I'm not sure the doctor would have agreed that this was restful activity what with those suitcases and all the pretty girls I encountered at the hotel. When I wasn't working, I went swimming in the hotel's pool or found a good spot to stretch out on the beach. The doctor would have liked that, I figured. The only problem was that I kept meeting so many nice young ladies, especially during Spring Break that I was getting pretty worn out. Soon I became anxious to be off to boot camp for some much-needed rest.

After the doctor cleared me for enlistment, I finished up my paperwork and went to Savannah, Georgia to be sworn in. While I was up there someone stole my motorbike. I then headed off to Parris Island, South Carolina for boot camp where the first thing I did was make out an allotment to send most of my pay home to my mother. I wrote her to try and save as much of it as possible so I could go on to school after my hitch was up. My next twelve weeks were packed full of many new experiences and intense basic training, most of which I thoroughly enjoyed.

Parris Island boot camp

Marine Boot Camp
The Making of a Marine
Parris Island to Hawaii

It would take more than simply entering the Corps to turn me into a Marine. That process required twelve grueling weeks of basic training followed by a graduation from boot camp ceremony. But first, myself and a roomful of other somewhat doubtful recruits raised our right hands before the flag and repeated the Oath of Allegiance along with a Marine lieutenant on 28 May, 1941. I had ridden a bus up to Savannah, Georgia that morning to enlist and the following morning boarded a second bus headed for boot camp at Parris Island, South Carolina.

We didn't really know what to expect but had all heard stories, some of them pretty alarming and several among us were downright fearful. I think I was a little better prepared then many of the other men due to my experiences up to that time and I was looking forward to yet another big adventure. Some of the Drill Instructors were loud and profane and began shouting the minute we arrived. Our DI proved fully capable of such behavior but he normally was coolly quiet, seldom even raising his voice. This tactic was much more effective than all the shouting imaginable. He usually didn't even speak directly to us but had a burly corporal relay his instructions. When he did speak, woe upon any recruit who failed to hear and immediately heed his words. I was to learn nearly everything I needed to succeed in the Marine Corps during those twelve weeks of basic training. After that everything else was just practice and reinforcement of what I had acquired there. Of course, some advanced technical training and special weapons instruction did come later.

Boot camp taught us to conform and to work and think as one. A recruit who failed to learn this lesson could not graduate but there were surprisingly few that didn't make it. Only genuine nonconformists or misfits failed to be molded by the tough training schedule. Nearly every recruit who started out graduated, although boot camp is specifically designed to eliminate those few who aren't cut out for Corps life. The Marines' strict and unforgiving code makes very few allowances for personal needs or desires. The Corps believes it's better to discover shortcomings during training rather than later in combat when lives are at stake. At the

29

same time, it prides itself on usually being able to overcome any obstacle and make worthwhile Marines out of almost every recruit. The dropout rate from Marine boot camp is extremely low because our most important lesson learned early on was that we were members of an elite team, a unit that never failed at anything it undertook.

In some cases in the early part of the twentieth century, young men entered the service as an alternative to jail. *"So, you don't think you would care for prison, eh? In that case I'm sure you'll be thankful for this opportunity to enlist in the military, serve your country and make something of yourself."* Words like these handed down from a judge's bench often rescued men from striped suits and prison food. *"As luck would have it, young man, the recruiter's office is right down the hall. Quite a coincidence, isn't it?"* It was by design, not accident that most Armed Forces recruiting offices were located in courthouses.

Whether a man joined due to patriotic zeal, economic need or even to avoid detention, most went on to later become successful. Early problems such as a lack of education and other obstacles usually proved no barrier once a man was in the Corps and often it was these very memories of hardships that provided extra incentives to succeed. When asked later what contributed most to their successes, many men pointed with pride to their early misfortunes coupled with the tough principles learned in boot camp.

In a play on words, Zell Miller, who came from a troubled youth himself, served in the Corps then went on to become a public servant and well-known author expressed this idea very well in the title of his book. Miller, who served as governor of Georgia before representing that state in the U.S. Senate, listed the benefits to be gained from Marine Corps training and discipline in his book called *"Corps Values: Everything You Need to Know I Learned in the Marines."*

The Corps prides itself on a sure cure for anyone who has trouble rising early. DI's and their assistants have developed the science of waking up sleepy recruits to a fine art form. The first indication that it's time to wake up is when the bright overhead lights hit you directly in the eyes. *"OK, hit the deck! Rise and shine. Get off your dead backsides and on your dying feet!"* These orders were often accompanied by the sound of a heavy glass Coca-Cola bottle scraping the inside ridges of a fifty-gallon "GI" garbage can.

This sound always brought ninety-eight percent of the sleepers tumbling out of their racks and into their clothes, leaving only that one guy who can sleep through anything. For this unlucky recruit, the corporal reserved his "special treatment." Grabbing one corner of the mattress he flipped the sleeping recruit high into the air. Thud! The sound of our sleeper hitting the stone-hard barracks floor made every one of us silently vow to sleep even more lightly in the future. Wide awake now, the recruit sat up and looked around while a vague aura of comprehension crept over him. Then he painfully jumped up and rushed to dress and get outside. It was not good to be the last man to arrive anywhere and he didn't want any more special attention. The Corps has little use for a recruit who is last at anything and often uses some very unpleasant ways of expressing this displeasure.

Miller's book recalls in particular that punctuality was next to Godliness in his platoon and relates how he learned that valuable lesson. *"I got the point directly as the tip of my DI's boot was applied forcefully to the seat of my pants the first time I was the last member of my platoon to finish a meal. We were allowed fifteen minutes to eat, clean and stack our stainless steel trays, then fall out into formation in front of the mess hall. The application of our instructor's boot was the undeviating penalty given three times a day for the last one to show up anywhere."* My DI never resorted to such tactics because he didn't have to. A word was enough.

I recently spent an enjoyable afternoon with Dan Jones, USMC, reminiscing about our boot camp days. Dan entered the Corps later than I and saw action in Vietnam but we found that our boot camp experiences were very similar. He is an artist now who works at his shop on Indian Trail near Atlanta making military and aviation art. Military collectors from all over the country value his shadow boxes for medals, military logos on flight jackets and war memorabilia. He surprised me by pulling out a book I hadn't seen for many years, a 1940 edition of "The Marine's Handbook." Every recruit had his own personal copy of this book in boot camp. Mine was the 7th Edition but when Dan opened his copy, which was published decades later we were amazed at how similar the two books were. Weapons were different, of course, a 1903 Springfield versus an M-16, but many other sections were nearly identical.

Dan and I also compared notes on things such as blackening rifle sights to cut down on glare for more accuracy and other marksmanship tips. The sections on hand grenades were very similar and some others hadn't changed at all. There is still a section on "bowel elimination," proving that the Corps strives to control every aspect of a recruit's life in boot camp. There is also still a section on vermin, which gives advice on how to get rid of body and pubic lice, guidance that failed to get the job done for me during my weeks at boot camp.

These days, physical punishment is not allowed in the training of recruits. I'm sure some instructors consider this a handicap, but most DIs are still masters of psychological intimidation and use it as a reliable tool for maintaining discipline. Many a recruit has been overheard to complain, *"I wish they would just go ahead and beat the heck out of me and leave my mind alone."* My own DI never resorted to physical force to make a point because he didn't have to. I don't know what it was about the man but he was an old China Marine, an especially tough breed and could make you feel like a whipped puppy with just a look. He had a complete mastery of an old-time Marine's full range of profanity but seldom resorted to it. All he need do was gaze at you in his special way and you were done for. On the rare occasions when that didn't work, a few choice words would quickly finish you off. I don't know what special power he had, but it was extremely effective. China Marines and other "Old Hands" who had been in for some years were the backbone of the Corps and their experience was especially valuable once the fighting started.

Physical conditioning training was extremely tough at Basic, but fortunately, I was in good shape from all that swimming and time spent on the chinning bar. I don't recall any actual difficulties with PT, although many recruits really struggled to pass the tests. Something did get to me in a big way, and that was the swamps. Boggy swamps are plentiful near Parris Island and nothing gave our instructors more pleasure than falling us out in the middle of the night and herding us into those murky hellholes. Visions danced through our heads of poisonous snakes, venom-filled insects and large alligators all waiting to get a crack at us. I never saw any large creatures and it wasn't really the swamps that bothered me but one tiny pest made us all miserable, a louse. This nearly microscopic insect caused me more discomfort than I could ever remember suffering before or since. I would come in from a night spent wading and floundering in the swamps with the worst case of crab lice imaginable. I showered in scalding hot water, scrubbed until I was raw and even shaved off all my body hair but they still tormented me. Finally the doctor gave me something akin to Campho-phonique, which gave me a little relief until it was time to wade back into the swampland again.

On nights when we were spared the swamps, there were other forms of entertainment. Our instructors especially enjoyed flipping on the lights in the wee hours to the tune of the GI can's disquieting noise, then dumping our footlockers upside down on the floor so we could spend the rest of the night making everything shipshape again. It was just a little prank called sleep deprivation that the instructors used to toughen us up.

Many values are first introduced to Marines or reinforced at boot camp. The list is endless but includes neatness, pride, being on time, courage, respect, brotherhood, discipline, perseverance, dependability and loyalty. There is one more, which I think should head the list but it's such a part of the Corps and so deep-seated in everything they do it's often taken for granted. Honor tops the list and is built into every Marine's training and being.

I recently met Navy man Carl Brashear, whose life was portrayed in the movie, "Men of Honor." U.S. Navy Master Chief Brashear was the first African-American to claim that title. Divers are a small exclusive group, and a black man was less than welcome back when Carl showed up for training. He confronted impossible odds of racism as well as numerous rugged physical challenges and overcame them all. For him also, the most important element in the military is Honor. He gained the master diver's title after losing a leg, an impossible achievement according to the Navy brass who tried to stand in his way. I felt an immediate bond with Master Chief Brashear. Sticking with it to the end and Honor are his watchwords. If you haven't seen the movie "Men of Honor," based on his life, don't miss it.

While I recall boot camp with many fond memories and enjoyed nearly everything, some others remember it quite differently. To some the DI was a demon and the cruelest of mentors. Many Marines were convinced their instructor's job was to make an enemy in battle appear like "a piece of cake" by comparison to boot training. Recruit instruction for some becomes a struggle to survive and endure and sometimes humor is the only way to maintain one's sanity. There are dozens of jokes and stories about recruit training and one favorite concerns a young man who decided to be part of the small percentage that leaves boot camp early. One afternoon he turned up missing and his DI was outraged. He had never lost a recruit and wasn't about to start now. *"Get out there and find him,"* he ordered his corporal. *"Take every man with you, comb the area until you turn him up, then bring Mr. Runaway back here to me. I want to talk to him."*

It was well into the night when the recruit was finally discovered, huddled in some bushes at the edge of a swamp and quickly brought before the DI. *"Why did you desert my training platoon?"* the DI demanded. *"Were you trying to destroy my perfect record? Do you hate your Drill Instructor? Well, do you?"*

"Sir, I can explain," whimpered the frightened young man. *"On my first day here I was issued a comb. Right after that, they took me to the barber and shaved my head."*

"So? Nobody but a coward would run over something like that," sneered the sergeant.

"On the second day," continued the recruit, *"I was issued a tooth brush after which I was marched to the dentist who proceeded to yank out most of my teeth."*

"A real man wouldn't let a little thing like that bother him," scoffed the DI.

"Yes Sir," continued the recruit, *"but yesterday when they issued me that athletic supporter, I decided not to stay around to find out what they would take away next."*

In boot camp the recruit is introduced to his rifle, his constant companion from that day forth. Every Marine is, before all else, a rifleman. The earliest Marines were recruited from sailors who happened to be exceptional marksmen. Sent up into the rigging of sailing ships, they fired down on the enemy with muskets. They were very efficient at this, often doing as much damage as the naval gunners did with their big cannons.

Whether the rifle is an M-1, a carbine, Garrand, M-16, or a Model 1903 Springfield like my first rifle was, it is always a Marine's best friend and closest companion. One Marine wrote a tribute that sums it up quite well:

This is my rifle, there are many like it, but this one is mine.

My rifle is not only my best friend, it is my very life. I must master it as I master my life.

My rifle, without me, is useless. Without it, I am useless. I must fire my rifle straighter than any enemy who is trying to kill me. I must shoot him before he shoots me, and I will.

My rifle and I both know that what counts is not the number of rounds, the length of the burst, nor the smoke and noise that we make. The only thing that really matters is the number of direct hits upon the enemy.

My rifle is as human as I am, because it is my life. Thus I will treat it like a brother. I will memorize its sights and barrel, strengths and weaknesses, every part and accessory. I will guard it against the ravages of weather and damage, as I also guard my own arms, eyes and heart against the enemy. I will keep it clean and ready. We will become part of each other.

Before God, I swear this oath to my rifle. Together we will defend our country and master all enemies. Together we are the saviors of my country and my life.

It shall be so until America's final victory over all enemies, until there are no foes remaining and peace reigns at last. -
Author Unknown.

Many boot camp routines began long before my era and remain much the same today, while others have changed considerably. Marines have done calisthenics and marched, marched, marched from earliest times, but another war called a "police action," in Korea introduced fighting men to "brainwashing" a Communist art that resulted in the American "Code of Conduct."

Code of Conduct

I.   I am an American, fighting in the forces which guard my country and our way of life. I am prepared to give my life in their defense.

II.   I will never surrender of my own free will. If in command, I will never surrender the members of my command while they still have the means to resist.

III.   If I am captured I will continue to resist by all means available. I will make every effort to escape and to aid others to escape. I will accept neither parole nor special favors from the enemy.

IV.   If I become a prisoner of war, I will keep faith with my fellow prisoners. I will give no information or take part in any action that might be harmful to my comrades. If I am senior, I will take command. If not, I will obey the lawful orders of those appointed over me and will back them up in every way.

V.   When questioned, should I become a prisoner of war, I am required to give only name, rank, service number, and date of birth. I will evade answering further questions to the utmost of my ability. I will make no oral or written statements disloyal to my country and its allies or harmful to their cause.

VI.   I will never forget that I am an American, fighting for freedom, responsible for my actions, and dedicated to the principles which made my country free. I will trust in my God and in the United States of America.

Nearly everything at boot camp is performed in unison and marching and calisthenics are no exceptions. The Corps believes this helps build a sense of unity and brotherhood in the troops. Exercises are usually done before breakfast, a meal many recruits are convinced is served in the middle of the night. This is an exaggeration because it is already nearly dawn before calisthenics time rolls around. The exercises include push-ups, sit-ups, deep knee bends and the famous squat-thrust, a jump from the prone position to a crouch and then on up to a standing posture. Don't try this one unless you are in really good shape or crazy.

Individual calisthenics are reserved as punishment for minor infractions of the many rules. During the first few boot camp days any mistake might result in something like; *"Drop and give me twenty!"* The recruit, being new, might not know what is expected at this stage and reply, *"Twenty what, sir?"* At this point he or she will most likely be severely chastised for their ignorance.

"Push-ups, you moron! When I say drop and give me twenty, you reply, 'Yes sir, hit the deck and give me twenty perfect push-ups, get it?"

"Yes Sir!"

"Good, now we're getting somewhere. Now, give me forty!"

"Forty, sir?"

"Are you questioning my orders? Give me fifty!"

Marine recruits become fit and savvy in a hurry. They march everywhere and the Regimental Commander is responsible for ensuring that all close order drill is properly conducted. If he has any questions he can refer to a book called, "The Marine Corps Recruit Depot Drill Manual." It consists of nearly four hundred pages and covers all marching, drill and ceremonies. Marching is judged literally every step of the way and all close order drill, parades and ceremonies are carefully evaluated as well.

Drilling is supervised, graded and monitored by the Regimental Drillmaster with the aid of Drill Instructors for Recruit platoons and DI School Instructors working with their students. There is a lot of marching and monitoring going on at any given moment. Not only recruits, but also the drill instructors are under observation while doing close order drill. He or she has to set an example for the recruits at all times. They must study the manual and become intimately familiar with such terms as element, formation, line, rank, column and file.

After mastering four hundred pages of this type of information, a DI is ready to drill his recruits. He now knows terms such as flank, depth, front, distance, interval, alignment, base, guide, point of rest, center, head, pace, step, cadence, quick time, double time, slow time, left and right dress, mass formation, parade sling, extended mass formation, piece, snap and many, many more.

The hundreds of pages cover every movement and contingency. Anyone who has completed recruit training remembers drilling with and without "pieces." The Manual of Arms for marching with a rifle is also included in the drill manual. Former recruits recall dreaming at night about; *"Right Shoulder Arms! Left Shoulder Arms! Present Arms! Right Face! Left Face! Forward March! To The Rear March!"* Dozens of such rapid-fire instructions are given over and over, each delivered in a voice sounding like it comes straight from the depths of hell. It takes Drill Instructors some time to develop their "drill voices," and several pages in the manual are also devoted to this special skill.

Small arms training took up a good portion of my 12 weeks. We made numerous trips to the firing range to qualify with the Springfield. It was a very fine and accurate weapon in spite of its age and is still favored by some target shooters today. Then I qualified with the .45 caliber pistol and made sharpshooter with both weapons. I don't know if my hours of nighttime practice out on that deserted Florida road with Jim and my .22 rifle helped or not, but it could have.

Just how tough boot camp can be is illustrated by a strange incident that took place in 1997. Riddick Bowe, heavyweight boxing contender, went toe-to-toe with then-champion Evander Holyfield on three occasions. He also fought brawler Andrew Golata twice and was considered a very tough guy by most boxing experts. Having some trouble staying is shape, Bowe decided to join the Marine Corps Reserve program and go through boot camp to toughen himself up and lose a little flab. He gave up after just eleven days and according to the Washington Post was ready to return to civilian life after the very first morning. For most Marines, it came as no surprise that a big, tough guy like Bowe could have trouble with boot camp, but for civilians who see the Corps as something between Gomer Pyle and "Full Metal Jacket," it came as a shock when he washed out.

Marine Gunnery Sergeant Wiley Tiller remarked at the time that boot camp is less about muscles than mental toughness. *"It would have been a big culture shock for Bowe, from the first moment he stepped off the bus, even though he was a trained athlete," said Tiller. "A coach yelling at you is nothing compared to your DI. The Corps strips you of anything you ever were and then builds you back up into what they want you to be. For a heavyweight fighter, that probably messed with his mind. The physical training was probably no harder than his boxing training, but being told what to do, how to do it, that would have been rough for a guy nearly thirty who's been through what Bowe has. What was missing might have depressed him even more. There would have been no entourages, no private showers or rooms, no special foods, no allowances made just because he was Riddick Bowe. He was simply another recruit and that would have been tough for him to take."*

Other Marines believe that if Bowe lacked the discipline and mental toughness to complete basic training, he might also lack what it takes to resurrect his boxing career and they also point out that he can't claim the title of Marine, even for those eleven days. *"When you graduate, that's when you become a Marine,"* said one NCO. *"When you walk in, and all the way through recruit training, you're nothing."* As one Army reporter put it, *"The Few,"* are Bowe's chances at another heavyweight title, *"The Proud,"* his refusal to quit in the ring in spite of declining condition and ability, and *"The Marines,"* a dream he will never fulfill.

After three months of intensive training, I emerged from the gates at Parris Island, a new Marine private headed, not to join a combat unit, but to Water Engineering School at Quantico, Virginia. The training would be similar to the work I had done with water heaters back in Florida and I looked forward to it. I don't know why they picked me to go to this particular school, and of course I didn't ask. If I had learned one thing in the past twelve weeks it was, when a Marine gets an order, he replies, *"Sir, yes sir!"* Then he does his absolute best to carry out that order. This part of our training proved very valuable to us later on in combat in the Pacific. If an order happens to be pleasing as this one was, you consider yourself very lucky.

The school, while similar to my water heater work, taught me a lot of new techniques and equipment and many more pipes and fittings and I enjoyed every minute of it. When weekend liberty was granted, I often took a train up to the capitol to take in the sights. I always caught the last train back just in time for Monday morning classes and was dead tired all day long.

Marines normally found out what was expected of them in one of two ways. Either someone senior told us about it or we received written orders posted on the bulletin board. After finishing my seven-week course, I spent a few more days at Quantico during which I was to receive both types of orders.

"All right, fall out! It's time for a little more training!" The corporal smiled in an evil way and we knew that couldn't be a good sign. After nearly five months of training, we couldn't think of a bit more training we

might need, but Marines follow orders so we fell out between the barracks. For the next few hours, a sergeant highly skilled in karate demonstrated that we weren't quite as tough as we might have imagined. First he showed us a maneuver, then asked for a volunteer, usually the biggest man in sight, who he then threw around like a rag doll for a few minutes, stopping just short of a killing thrust. It was one time I was glad to be one of the smaller Marines because I didn't get picked. Then we practiced on each other. We enjoyed this training and it made me remember my boxer friend Jeff. We also felt sure it might come in handy later on.

Next day I found an order posted on the board and learned I was one of eight graduates selected to go to Pearl Harbor, Hawaii and join the 3rd Defense Battalion. We were all privates and had enlisted at about the same time. I was told I was in charge for the train ride from Quantico to Washington, D.C., and then for the four-day trip to northern California. I would handle meal vouchers, train tickets and so forth. I wasn't the senior man but my name started with the first letter of the alphabet, so I was elected. We reached Washington D.C., entered the train station and, with a little time before boarding, went to a big open balcony overlooking a residential street below. All of a sudden we heard "Bam! Bam!" Two men crouched behind a car were firing at some policemen down behind another car. "Bang! Bang!" The policemen returned fire. It was quite a show but our boarding call came right then and we didn't get to see how things turned out.

I took care of finding our bunks and so forth while keeping an eye out because I knew I would be blamed if anything went wrong. After a long four-day ride, the train dropped us at a huge train station in San Francisco. We reported to the Duty Sergeant at Mare Island Naval Base and learned our ride to Hawaii would be on the USS Lexington, an aircraft carrier bound for duty in the Pacific. We soon got underway from Mare Island and I soon discovered I had never seen anything like this massive ship. I got a great view of the Golden Gate Bridge as we passed right under it. Next I saw a big island with gray buildings, which I learned was called Alcatraz. It looked like a very desolate and uninviting place.

The carrier was very lively and interesting. There was a large detachment of marines aboard whose primary job was shipboard security. They also ran the brig, marched prisoners to and fro and manned anti-aircraft gun positions during General Quarters. The ship had a huge water distillation system that provided fresh water at sea and when the navy engineers found out about us they offered to give us all a tour of their plant. It was much bigger than those we had studied in school and we were greatly impressed but tried not to show it. After all, we were water engineers too.

We usually stayed pretty close to our quarters because every time we wandered around the ship, we got lost. An aircraft carrier is like one giant maze and it takes a long time to figure out how to find your way from place to place. If you get lost you tend to stay lost unless lucky enough to spot a ship's company Marine. Otherwise you asked a sailor, often getting a look expressing clearly what he thought of having passengers aboard his ship.

A carrier is much like a small city with its own public works, hospital, churches, service stations, restaurants, police force and a jail called the brig. Police duties are divided between the Marine Detachment and ship's company sailors called Masters-at-Arms. Anyone who has been on a carrier remembers the sound made by a file of prisoners as Marine guards marched them from the brig to chow down on the mess decks or up onto the hangar deck for drilling and exercise. The prisoners, sailors who have broken ship's rules, are required to stomp down hard on the metal deck in marching cadence. The sound carries for long distances through the metal plating and is always accompanied by a Marine guard shouting; *"Make way! Prisoners coming through!"* The smart thing is to get out of the way quickly or you might get run down by angry prisoners or else "written up" by a guard.

The ship's captain is judge and jury for all minor shipboard discipline. These proceedings are called Captain's Mast and hail all the way back to early sailing days when offenders were tied to the mast to receive their prescribed number of lashes, sometimes being whipped to death for the more serious offenses. "Brig time" is the punishment for minor offenses now. Graver violations of military law go before a court-martial jury. The Naval Justice System when I was making the crossing was called "Rocks and Shoals." These regulations prescribed exact punishments for each offense and gave the ship's captain very little room to use his own discretion. AWOL, Absence Without Official Leave could be handled at Captain's Mast but its more serious counterpart, "Missing a Ship's Movement" called for a court-martial and punishment was usually severe. Missing ship's departure or any other military movement is an unforgivable violation anytime but it can bring the death penalty in wartime. Lesser offenses ran from dereliction of duty to insubordination. A ship's captain could put a man away for quite a while and might also prescribe a diet of bread and water, a much more severe punishment than one might imagine.

Once at sea, the *"Lex"* went right to work. This wasn't to be a luxury cruise and regularly the big ship shuddered as she turned into the wind for flight operations. It's much easier to launch an airplane into the wind and while a big airport switches runways to take advantage of the wind, at sea a ship must turn. It was quite a spectacular show as planes took off and were recovered and as I watched I decided I would some day like to learn to fly. "General Quarters" sounded often and sailors quickly manned their gunnery stations. Captain and crew took their duties and the ship's state of readiness very seriously.

In a few days we arrived at Pearl Harbor and reported directly to the 3rd Defense Battalion on the U.S. Naval Station where another man and myself were assigned to "G" Battery. Next morning at Roll Call a sharp-looking young Marine officer addressed us. This was my first meeting with the man I would have a life-long association with, First Lieutenant, General-to-be, Howard G. Kirgis, U.S.M.C. He stood before us, looking sharp, like an "Annapolis man," who didn't quite know what to do with his two new water engineers. He looked us over and must have been satisfied with what he saw because he said, *"You two are water engineering school graduates but I can't imagine what we need with even one water engineer. I'm going to assign you new jobs here, but since you've graduated from technical school, I'll also promote you both to Private First Class. Congratulations and welcome aboard."* I liked this young lieutenant already and not just because he had promoted me. He looked and acted like he knew exactly what he was doing and that gave us confidence. When he got promoted to Captain a few days later, we all felt good.

I was assigned to a searchlight crew. I was to be power plant operator, which meant I kept the generator that powered the searchlight in tip-top working condition. We spent the next few weeks training and pulling liberty and I began to really enjoy my new duty. Two events that took place about this time will be with me as long as I live. I met a Japanese girl that I really grew to care for in a short period of time and a friend of mine discovered that his sister was working downtown as a prostitute.

Mike slept just a few bunks down from me. One weekend he went to Honolulu on liberty and next I heard he was gone. A buddy who was with him told us what happened and it was a real tragedy. The two of them decided to go to a new little club that turned out to be a house of ill-repute where two dollars was the going price. The two Marines told the

Mama-San that they weren't interested in partaking of her wares and she took immediate offense. *"Just look! Look at my beautiful girls!"* she screamed and threw back a curtain behind which sat a dozen or so young women. *"Two girls tried to sit on our laps,"* our friend reported, *"but Mike suddenly went nuts. His eyes bugged out of their sockets and he grabbed one of the other girls shouting, 'What the hell are you doing in here? I should kill you!' Then he tried to dismantle that cathouse board by board. Soon the Shore Patrol showed up, cuffed him, and hauled him away."*

As it turned out, the girl was Mike's sister who had come over from the States to go into business for herself. Life can sure be rough. It wasn't long before they sent Mike back to the States and we never saw him again. I steered clear of those establishments. They were nothing but trouble and there were plenty of other sights to see in Honolulu, including countless pretty girls. I nearly fell in love with one of them and if things had turned out differently I might still be with her.

I had met Jack soon after arriving. We became good friends and first chance we had headed off to see downtown Honolulu. While we were taking in the sights, we got hungry and started looking for something to eat. We spotted a sidewalk hotdog stand operated by a pretty young girl who was singing out in a musical voice, *"Get your doggies! Oh, get your hotdoggies here."* She was quite popular and we lined up behind several people.

As luck would have it, we were right behind two pretty young oriental girls, and one of them almost took my breath away with her good looks. I couldn't think how to start a conversation until I came up with the brilliant line, "Are these hot dogs any good?" They both giggled behind their hands and the one I liked claimed they were the best on the island. "In that case," I said, "I'll buy us all one and we can have lunch together." The girls giggled again and agreed, so we had a nice lunch and visit in a nearby park. I believe this was the first time I had ever spoken to an oriental person in my life. Her name was Mariko and she won my heart before the hotdogs were even half finished. Then we went on a tour with the girls showing us many interesting sights, like the beaches and a statue of a Hawaiian king. We also saw a row of stores, each with what looked like the assorted insides of various animals hanging out front, which made Jack and I begin to regret our hotdogs.

Before long it was time for us to return to base. I asked Mariko if I could take her to dinner the following night and she agreed and gave me her address and phone number. After dinner we went to a movie during which she told me she was from Japan and I told her that was fine with me and before we parted I made another date with her for the coming Friday night. We were out on night maneuvers all week and that was the soonest I could get back to town. Mariko and I quickly became great friends and I think I could have gotten really serious about her but fate had other plans for both of us. We knew nothing except that we really liked each other and had no hint at all that we would soon part, never to see each other again. In the days following the attack I couldn't locate Mariko. I tried to telephone her from the base as soon as I could but got no answer. I later went to her house but it looked empty and desolate. I went up to a neighbor's door to try and find some answers. What the neighbor told me left an empty place inside. *"Mariko and her family are prisoners of war. They rounded up anybody that had been to Japan in the past 6 months or had duel citizenship and put them all in detention camps. You can't even see them,"* She said sadly. I vowed to try and find Mariko and her family but I was soon shipped out and never saw her again. I still sometimes think of her.

Less than two months after I arrived at Pearl, we found ourselves trying to fight off attacking Japanese planes with only small arms fire, but my battalion had been formed two years earlier at Parris Island and boasted a very rich history. Following the war, General Kirgis and others were called upon to share our outfit's story. I include part of it here for background and hope you will enjoy it along with the menu from their final cruise dinner upon reaching Hawaii, something I found quite interesting.

In the words of Howard G. Kirgis, Brigadier General, United States Marine Corps Retired; *"The Third Defense Battalion was the first ground unit to be deployed in the Pacific Area in anticipation of hostile action there during World War II. It was also the only unit to see continuous action on Guadalcanal from start to finish."*

The 3rd Defense Battalion was formed on October 10, 1939 as a unit of the 1st Marine Brigade at Parris Island, South Carolina. Corps officials drew nearly 1,000 personnel from the 15th Marines for this purpose. On December 1, 1939, the Battalion was detached from the brigade and assigned to the Fleet Marine Force. Four months of training and preparation for departure to Pearl Harbor followed, then on April 4, 1940 the Battalion embarked aboard the *USS Chaumont*, Commander Oliver O. Kessing, serving as captain. It took more than a month to reach Pearl Harbor after stops at Charleston, S.C., Guantanamo Bay, Cuba,

Cristobal and Balboa, Canal Zone plus a four-day layover in San Diego before beginning the eight-day Pacific crossing.

The farewell dinner held just before landing on Sunday, 5 May was attended by the battalion's officers and families including seventeen children listed on the program as "Miss" or "Master." The dinner menu is interesting, if a bit curious by today's standards and was made up of: Salted Almonds and Peanuts, Macadamia Nuts, Pickled Watermelon, Chilled Tomato Juice, Assorted Canapé, Curled Celery, Queen Olives, Sylmar Ripe Olives, Consomme' and Saltines. The Main Course consisted of Fillet of Fletan-Chesterfield, Roll Romona Dindon, Huitre Dressing, Abatis Gravy, and Canneberge Sauce. Then came Sweet Pomme de Terre-Marshmallow, followed by Petit Pois, Sally Lynn-Confiture, Salad a' la Jardiniere, Mayonnaise, Miracle Whip, or French Dressing. Next was Fromage: Roquefort, Swiss, Pimento, and Crème. Last came the Desserts: Vanilla Ice Cream, Chocolate Sauce, Cake, Fruit Sauce, Fudge, plus Café' Noir and Cigarettes. The seventeen young masters and misses were spared the black coffee and cigarettes and probably the evening's movie featuring Joan Crawford, Robert Taylor and Franchot Tone, "The Gorgeous Hussy." Life could often get tedious on a sea voyage of more than 7,000 nautical miles, and a good final meal and movie were to be appreciated.

Included on the List of Passengers was Kirgis, Howard G., 1st Lt. USMC, more than a year away from becoming my boss and a captain. General Kirgis and I were to become life-long friends and I was very saddened by his recent death.

The 3rd Defense Battalion arrived in Pearl Harbor, Territory of Hawaii on 7 May 1940 and was tasked to protect resources on Oahu and prepare for further deployment to the far reaches of the Pacific. The winds of war would soon sweep what was later called "The Pacific Theater" and the 3rd Defense was the first unit to be deployed in anticipation of possible hostilities. In September 1940, an advance 3rd Defense detachment of 400 men was sent to Midway Island, which would be their home for the next year. Nearly 600 more Marines, the remainder of the battalion joined the advance party in February 1941 and brought it to normal strength of nearly 1,000 officers and men. This was eight months before I joined the unit. Their mission was to install defenses on Midway and occupy them until relieved. This was ten months before the attack on Pearl Harbor and sixteen months prior to the all-out assault on Midway by a major Japanese task force in June of 1942. Japan's objective at Midway was to secure a base for use as a staging point for a second attack on Pearl Harbor and other Pacific bases. I had wound up on Midway by this time, following a roundabout route.

In early October 1941 the 6th Defense Battalion relieved the 3rd Defense on Midway, and our battalion then returned to Pearl Harbor for a well-earned period of "Rest and Relaxation" mixed with light training. This is when I arrived to find the men dividing their time between cleaning and replacing equipment, light night training maneuvers and R&R. Anyone who has had duty on remote Pacific islands knows that, after eight months on Midway, they deserved some time off. Some units of the 3rd returned to Midway with 3" AA guns to reinforce the 6th Bn and were present for the Battle of Midway. I arrived in time for that too, by an unusual set of circumstances. I had been separated from my unit and was on Midway serving in my specialty as water engineer when the Japanese attacked. Unknown to me, Midway's fresh water supply was to play a major role in our eventual success in the battle, but I knew nothing about that at the time.

In July of 1942, the battalion sailed off for Guadalcanal to join the 1st Marine Division for an amphibious assault there and I was with them. Very few Pacific engagements failed to find at least part of the 3rd involved. In addition to the battles covered in this book, they also saw action at Bougainville, Tassafaronga, Kukum, Kokumbona and Puruata, to mention but a few. By June of 1944, the outfit was so split up that the bulk of it was redesignated the 3rd AA Battalion and attached to the III Amphibious Corps Artillery. The 3rd Defense Battalion took part in the battle at Pearl Harbor on December 7th 1941, the Battle of Midway on 4 June 1942 and the Guadalcanal-Tulagi landings 7-9 August 1942. They stayed on to help capture and then defend Guadalcanal and Tulagi from August '43- February '44.

They also took part in Consolidation of the Northern Solomons, December '43 - June '44, and the occupation and defense of Cape Torokina. We participated in the assault on Saipan and Tinian, followed by several months fighting there near the end of the war. Our unit also saw action later in the Philippines and served on Mainland Japan during the occupation. The Korean War saw many of our men still in uniform and in the thick of the action. The battalion received the Navy Unit Commendation for duty on Midway, but I don't want to be getting ahead of my story.

One interesting event took place about the time I got to Hawaii and it really shocked me. It also pleased me more than I could have hoped for. My parents both divorced their new spouses and got back together, and it was just after Pearl Harbor when I received the amazing news that they had remarried. I think they always loved each other but I guess they needed to mature a little. This type of behavior was just about unheard of in those days but my parents were always unconventional people. Whatever their reasons, they had done it and I was very happy to hear about it.

My father served in World War I and spent extensive time on the front lines in Europe, so the Army now decided they badly needed him back. He enlisted as soon as war was declared and they sent him straight to officer's training school where he became a lieutenant. They needed men with experience and soon sent him to Walla-Walla Army Air Station in Washington State where he served as Provost Marshall, a sort of military sheriff. My mother went to welder's school and then worked at a nearby aircraft plant. Many women filled those "Rosie-the-Riveter" type jobs, especially after the war started and the draft and enlistments drained the labor market of most able-bodied men. I wanted to see them both as soon as possible but it would be quite some time before that was possible. Events beyond our control were to keep us apart for more than a year.

Prelude to Pearl
The Plans Before the Storm

As early as June 1931, all cadets graduating from the Japanese Imperial Naval Academy were asked the same question on their final examination, and what an engaging question it was. *"Please write in your own words how you would attack and defeat the military forces of the United States of America, concentrating on the Pacific and especially the naval forces at Pearl Harbor, Territory of Hawaii."*

The question came as no surprise to the cadets. When not studying seamanship, weaponry or naval history, they often discussed such topics with their instructors in class. Later, alone in their dorms or at the academy library, they studied maps and held spirited debates among themselves over the conquest of many foreign territories including the United States. Battle was in their blood because they considered themselves Samurai warriors. Japanese military men of all ranks claimed the honor of belonging to this warrior class and also saw themselves as children of their emperor. The emperor, for his part, was divine, a direct descendent of Japanese Sun Goddess Amaterasu O-Mi-Kami. She was one of the earliest goddesses of Shinto, the national religion of most Japanese. The warrior's way was, for these men, the only honorable path to follow.

Japanese history is rich with stories and legends of heroic warfare and self-sacrifice. Tales of the thirteen Ronin, forerunners to the Ninjas, and other heroes of Japanese legends were usually war stories with very sad endings. The heroes almost always died at the story's conclusion, often by their own hands to atone for some real or imagined mistake. The only honorable way a member of Japanese aristocracy, man or woman, could save face was by committing hara-kiri, more correctly known as seppuku. This ritual suicide makes use of the shorter of the Samurai's two swords. The person intent upon on death kneels on a rug after much prayer and sake drinking aimed at stiffening their resolve. A friend usually stands by holding the longer Samurai sword. The plan is to drive the shorter sword deep into the bowels, jerk upward with a killing motion hopefully severing major organs and arteries. The second's duty is to stand by watchfully and not allow the victim to linger in agony or falter in courage. Either action brings a swift deadly stroke of the razor-edged larger sword. If the strike is perfect, heads literally roll. Toward the end of the Second World War, military suicides were so common there were not enough swords to handle the volume and many were forced to use a pistol instead. Japanese civilians on the colonized islands also leaped to their deaths from towering cliffs, often with children clutched tightly to their bosoms. When approaching one island, our landing craft could hardly make way because of the bodies floating in the surf.

Japan's earliest battles were fought between warring factions within her own borders but in the nineteenth and twentieth centuries she began exporting war to her Asian neighbors. The modern Japanese soldier still embodied many of the Samurai's warlike characteristics even though his weapons had changed. Samurai believed that any enemy who was captured alive or surrendered was below contempt and should be dealt with more like an animal than a human being. It was dishonorable to be taken alive. One must always fight to the death and this belief was to result in terrible atrocities being committed against Japan's prisoners of war.

Japanese cadets in the 1930s considered themselves traditional Samurai but many also wanted to become modern airmen. They dutifully studied seamanship, as required but many also dreamed of becoming pilots. They believed air power would determine the outcome of future wars. In this their thoughts ran parallel to an American air-minded sailor, a Navy admiral named Yarnell. The difference was that Yarnell was soon to prove his theory, to the guidance and delight of the Japanese military.

"*Bombs,*" read the would-be airmen's papers, "*along with torpedoes and bullets fired from carrier-launched aircraft, destroying American ships and aircraft. Then we would demolish fuel supplies, ground personnel and other important structures. After these first strikes at Pearl Harbor, we also suggest launching similar attacks against the Philippines and Guam, followed by amphibious assaults. Next should come an all-out invasion of the American homeland to subjugate the people to our Emperor's will. That is, respectfully, how to bring down the United States.*"

These cadets had obviously done their homework and some instructors found these papers quite fascinating. Other more traditionally minded faculty members were disturbed and offended and said so. "*It is the warrior on the ground, fighting face-to-face, hand-to-hand, that will decide all future wars,*" these traditionalists insisted, "*just as they have decided all battles in the past. Such warriors may travel into battle on ships and perhaps even in aircraft, but battles are to be fought on the ground, not soaring in the air. We believe that activity should be reserved for the birds.*"

Japan bellowed it's first roar of aggression with an invasion into China's northern neighbor, Manchuria in the early 1930s. While such invasions were not new in Japan's history, the large scale of this one was a first. Beginning in the late nineteenth century and on into the early twentieth Japan set out to dominate neighboring East Asian territories. The plan was to then expand throughout Asia and boldly occupy selected strategic areas, especially those rich in natural resources, always in short supply in the tiny island nation. Advances were only to be halted when confronted by strong resistance or threats of retaliation, something that seldom if ever occurred. In this way and also as a result of some lucky windfalls, the Empire steadily grew in size, strength and resources.

In 1894 Japan went to war against China for the first time. By defeating China and gaining present-day Taiwan, known then as Formosa for her efforts, Japan served notice that she was planning to expand in Asia. Ten years later in 1904, she challenged and defeated the Russians in China at Port Arthur, now called Lushun. This proved she was not afraid to tackle "a major power," and proved that Asians could best western or occidental nations. In 1910 she annexed the ancient kingdom of Korea, a country she had previously pledged to guard and protect. Japan was to employ this type of "annexation" in many of her dealings with other countries. Later takeovers were accomplished under the guise of something called, "The Greater East-Asian Co-prosperity Sphere".

In 1914 Japan entered at the last possible moment into what would later be called the First World War. Her allies were France and Great Britain and although her troops hardly fired a shot, Japan took possession of Tsingtao on the Shantung Peninsula, the German concession in China, the Carolines, including Truk, and the Palaus. She was also given the Marshall Islands and the Marianas, except for Guam and many hard-fought costly battles would later be needed to get them back. The United States had purchased Guam from the Spanish in 1899 at the close of the Spanish-American War and at the same time gained possession of the Philippine Islands, Puerto Rico and Guantamano Bay, in Cuba. The hold on Puerto Rico and "Gitmo Bay" has not been released to this day. The Philippines is now an independent nation but the United States experimented with its own brand of imperialism there for forty years after driving out the Spanish and putting down the bloody "Filipino Insurrection." During this much-criticized war at the turn of the twentieth century, American troops slaughtered a half-million Filipinos. The Spanish had dominated the Filipinos for hundreds of years but were about to be overrun and decapitated by angry bolo-brandishing natives led by Emilio Aguinaldo. The United States actually bought the Philippines from the Spanish and part of the deal was to offer them safe passage out of Manila and away from the angry Filipinos and their razor-sharp machetes.

The Japanese government made clear its plans for China early in the twentieth century. In 1915 they presented China with a list of unreasonable requests entitled the "Twenty-one Demands." It was clear from this document that Japan planned to make China nothing more than a colony. They demanded direct command over the Chinese military and full control of every aspect of Chinese life, political, industrial and agricultural, along with unlimited rights to use China's resources as they saw fit. The United States already had a plan for China called the "Open Door Policy," which was in direct conflict with these Japanese demands. This policy for Western conduct in the Far East had been agreed to by all major European powers and Japan had also signed it. In response to loud objections by both China and the West, Japan withdrew her demands for the time being but made secret plans to bide her time then reapply them again as soon as possible.

In 1919, at the Post-War Peace Conference, Japan acquired *"all former German possessions in the Pacific that lay north of the Equator."* Although many Western nations had interests in the Orient in the early 1900s, warning signs of impending conflict with Japan were everywhere. Most nations chose to maintain the status quo and ignore any threatening signs on the horizon. During the 1930s, when these nations were deep in a worldwide economic crisis called the "Great Depression," Japan took the opportunity to strike in China, this time with troops to back up her words.

As Japan invaded, Western powers grumbled but did nothing. This lack of action would later come back to haunt the West terribly. Half-hearted criticism by the League of Nations did nothing to discourage the Japanese. On the contrary, it prodded them to take even more aggressive action. Angry Japanese delegates stalked out of the League's assembly and before leaving Geneva, they gave formal notice of their intention to withdraw from the League entirely. The stage for major conflict was being set.

In 1934 the Japanese gave notice of their future intentions to the world. They declared they would no longer abide by the limitations of the Washington Naval Disarmament Treaty of 1922 and in 1937 they attacked China. This assault was designed both to test their still small but rapidly growing war machine's capabilities and to gauge the world's reactions. Japan was actually more curious than concerned about how the powerful nations of the West would respond to her long-range plans for Asian domination. Her soldiers were, after all, the invincible Samurai. Seeing no military opposition in her path, Japan pressed on with her conquests and plunged on toward her visualized destiny, to dominate Asia.

The lack of response to Japan's actions in China shocked many observers. Nobody, it seemed, wanted to take the chance of going to war with Japan and certainly not over China. The world was horrified, of course, by the countless atrocities committed by Japanese soldiers in the "Rape of Nanking." Still, America and the West took no military action against the Japanese. Even when Japanese airmen intentionally bombed, strafed and sank a United States gunboat on the Yangtze River, the only American response was irate lip service. Encouraged by these events, the Japanese began making plans for still more action in Asia, but they were not alone in this warlike activity. Other aggressors were at work elsewhere in the world and they applauded Japan's actions.

Germany and Italy had begun similar programs of territorial domination in Europe and Africa and they eagerly invited Japan to join them in a common cause of world conquest. The "Axis" powers signed a mutual assistance pact in 1937. This was meant to prevent any outside interference with their plans of world conquest. In August 1940, after the outbreak of war in Europe and the fall of France, Germany took positive steps to help the Japanese advance their interests in Asia even more. The Germans sent a strong "request" to the puppet French administration they had installed after the fall of Paris called the "Vichy Government."

Germany had learned early on in its conquests that it was better to administer vanquished countries by using local officials rather than Germans. Of course, these puppet regimes had every string pulled by their German masters and now the Germans forced the French to allow Japanese inroads into northern French Indo-China. This country shared a common border with China and offered a direct invasion route. Americans would come to know this little country by another name in the 1960s after it's people succeeded in driving French troops from their borders and America stepped in to try and fill the void. By this time the citizens had renamed their little country. They called it Vietnam.

The three predatory nations continued forging alliances. Less than a month after the Mutual Assistance Pact of 1937, they met once again. The result this time was called the "Tripartite Treaty of 27 September," a treaty which pledged combined action by all three Axis Powers should any of them go to war against the United States.

The United States had traditionally been a friend of China and an avid backer of the Open Door Policy, since just after the "Boxer Rebellion" at the turn of the twentieth century. They strongly opposed in principle Japan's movement to dominate the Chinese Republic. The time was right for the Japanese to act because China was already involved in an internal civil war. Communist guerrilla forces under Mao Tse-tung were arrayed against the Nationalist Chinese Army under General Chiang Kai-sheck. This conflict left the Chinese nation strife-torn and vulnerable. Strong sentiment by the majority of Americans during the late 1930s favored peace at all costs. The memory of the recent "War to End All Wars" in Europe was still fresh in everyone's mind and there was almost no support for any direct military action to save China or any other foreign government from outside aggression.

American citizens and the government of the United States alike were however, openly sympathetic to and supportive of China's plight. Moral outrage soon led to embargoes against munitions shipments to Japan, combined with ever-increasing amounts of material aid to China. Perhaps the most interesting development during this period was in the air over China. Volunteer American pilots were being relieved of their duties in the United States and permitted to train with the Chinese Air Force in preparation for air battle against the Japanese. Embargoes on the shipment of munitions to Japan were soon followed by much more stringent restrictions. Japan was dependent upon the United States for oil and scrap metal shipments because she had almost no raw materials of her own. This lack of resources to support a large population was the main driving reason behind Japan's territorial desires. The United States soon halted shipments of these materials as well, placing Japan in a desperate situation.

Two factors greatly encouraged Japan's actions in the late 1930s. One was the success of Hitler in Europe. As Germany and Italy invaded neighboring countries gobbling up raw materials and captive labor forces, Japan looked on hungrily, licking her chops. Germany placed ever-increasing pressure upon England, and each victory left more Europe-held Asian plums ripe for the Japanese to pluck. Military leaders began greedily planning to grab these territories as soon as possible. After assuring that much of China's support and foreign aid were cut off, the Japanese opened up their invasion routes through French Indo-China and advanced into China's vulnerable heartland. The campaign of takeovers was on.

After invading China against only token opposition, Japan became even bolder but needed an excuse to blame the Chinese for starting a war in order to lessen world opposition. To provoke the Chinese into open warfare, they staged an armed confrontation at the "Marco Polo Bridge." These first shots were fired between Chinese and Japanese troops in July near the small town of Wanping, just outside of Nanking. Claims of just who fired the first shots conflict, with some observers even blaming Mao who was anxious for the Japanese to strike and place additional pressure on the Nationalists.

Using the bridge incident as an excuse, Japan's invading forces lay siege to Nanking and took the city on December 13. Japanese soldiers committed terrible atrocities against both Chinese citizens and soldiers in the city and throughout the surrounding countryside. They also harassed foreign nationals and their military in an attempt to dislodge them from the International Settlements near Peking. The day before Nanking fell to the Japanese, either to test America's will to fight or to try and draw them into the war, sank a small American warship, the gunboat *Panay* in Chinese waters, killing and wounding several aboard. If their goal was to draw the Americans into open warfare, it failed. After some initial outrage, Americans again took a mute and isolated stance.

The Marco Polo Bridge Incident, The Rape of Nanking, and the sinking of the *USS Panay* were three events that set the stage for war in the Pacific. All three helped lead Japan to Pearl Harbor and are worth examining in some detail.

The Marco Polo Bridge, called "Luguoqiao," sits near the village of Wanping, not far from the heart of the walled city of Nanking. Built more than eight hundred years ago in 1192, the bridge has undergone many changes down through the centuries. The original arches were washed away in the seventeenth century in one of China's notorious great floods and the present-day bridge is a composite of many different eras. It was widened in 1969 to handle increased traffic crossing Wanping's river, the Yongding. Along the bridge's nearly one thousand-foot length are marble railings that support 485 carved stone lions. All who see the bridge agree it is an impressive sight.

During the Qing Dynasty, Emperor Qianlong did his best to make the original bridge famous in China, as its namesake Marco Polo did in Europe but it is this much more recent event for which the bridge will forever be known. In early July 1937, Japanese troops illegally occupied a railway junction near Wanping during a "training" exercise. A shot was fired, nobody can say for sure by whom but many more immediately followed from both sides of the bridge. Hostilities between Japan and China quickly broke out, sparked by this "shot heard around the world." It could have been the Japanese who fired first, under orders from their military extremist officers or the Nationalist Chinese soldiers manning the gatehouse could have fired the shot from nervousness. Whoever fired that first shot on July 7, 1937, the "China Incident," as it became known, opened the door for all-out war in China.

The American government, and especially President Franklin Delano Roosevelt and his Secretary of State Cordell Hull knew that the American people were not ready to go to war in support of China. There were two primary reasons for this. First, some Americans mistakenly felt that the Chinese who outnumbered the Japanese by more than eight-to-one should be able to take care of themselves. Second was the powerful and popular "America First Movement." Well-known citizens including Charles A. Lindbergh led the movement. When he flew the first solo crossing of the Atlantic in a tiny single-engine plane, Lindburg immediately became an American hero. Now his followers held rallies and parades to support "Lindy" and assure the government they wanted no part of war, in Europe or Asia.

Four years later, Roosevelt, always a keen politician, would be hoping for a "first strike" against America by the Japanese to unite the American people in a war effort. In 1937, however, even he was not ready for war. Roosevelt later got his wish, but it was a much more terrible strike than he had bargained for. Pearl Harbor went far beyond what he had foreseen, and nearly doomed the entire United States Pacific Fleet.

Five days after the Marco Polo Bridge incident, *USS Panay* rested at the bottom of the Yantze River, sunk by Japanese warplanes. With seeming sincerity and promptness the Japanese apologized, insisting the sinking had been a "tragic mistake" brought about by poor visibility. This was all the reassurance needed by most American people at the time. An inquiry held by U.S. Navy Admiral Yarnell two weeks later stopped just short of calling the Japanese liars. All the while insisting their pilots had not seen the American flags plastered all over the *Panay*, the Japanese promised to pay the American government an indemnity. They bowed low, formally apologized, and that put an end to it. The American government and people, it seemed, were willing at this point to turn a blind eye to almost any hostile act.

The following day, the Nationalist Chinese capitol city of Nanking fell, setting the stage for a Japanese military orgy of unsurpassed carnage, rape, and murder. This cowardly event, dubbed the "Rape of Nanking," rivaled the terrible Jewish Holocaust in brutality but was never as well documented.

By December 13, 1937 Japanese bombers had been softening up the city for several days. Opposing this daily battering was a small handful of fighter pilots flying an assortment of obsolete British, German, Italian and American planes. Former U. S. Army flying officer Claire Chennault had trained these pilots. He later became commander of an all-volunteer group of American flyers in China, the famous "Flying Tigers." Chennault had been invited to China by Chiang Kai-shek to organize an air force for the Nationalists, who already had their hands full fighting Chinese Communist forces while at the same time preparing to take on the Japanese. The more modern Japanese air forces overwhelmed Chennault's little group of planes and on December 13, Nanking fell. Japanese troops stormed into the city and every day for months afterward, the world was shocked to hear of their horrible and unprecedented savageness.

Panic raged through Nanking such as cannot be described or even imagined by civilized people. Sheer terror swept the streets of the ancient walled city as Chinese soldiers threw away anything that identified them with the military. Cast-off weapons and uniforms littered city streets as more and more soldiers donned peasant clothing and fled alongside terrified civilians. Thousands died attempting to scale city walls and escape by lowering themselves down the steep, sheer drop on the other side. Thousands more perished trying to cross the Yangtze when overcrowded junks and small boats capsized and sank.

As jubilant troops poured through the walls, they brought uncontrolled butchery the likes of which had never been witnessed. The carnage was inescapable as frightened Chinese who made the mistake of running were quickly shot or bayoneted and those who stood still faced an identical fate. There was just no way to escape the killing, rape and looting spree. Soldiers entered and ransacked the same houses over and over again as trembling occupants were robbed, beaten and raped repeatedly. Men suspected of being soldiers were tied together in groups and used for bayonet, sword, hand-grenade or small arms practice. If pressed for time or bored with their games of death, soldiers machine-gunned their helpless victims or doused them with gasoline and threw matches on them, so casually said some observers that it looked almost like an afterthought.

The Chinese already knew what to expect due to reports filtering in ahead from the countryside. The Japanese conquerors carved a path of rape, pillage and murder all the way from Shanghai and other points. The Chinese army was outnumbered more than two-to-one, exhausted, demoralized after retreating ahead of the advancing Japanese for many days. In addition the Japanese had more than 200 tanks, unlimited artillery and supplies, and a substantial fleet that by the second day had taken complete control of the Yangtze and blockaded Nanking. The fate of every citizen cowering inside what was left of the longest city wall in China was now sealed. Many dead Chinese were found holding leaflets tightly clutched in their hands. The Japanese had dropped thousands of these promising "preferential treatment" and employment to any Chinese citizen, especially soldiers, who surrendered voluntarily. Terrified Chinese must have read the final words at the bottom with vain hope; "Japanese troops will exert themselves to the utmost to protect good citizens and enable them to live in peace, enjoying their occupations."

The invading troops were clearly exerting themselves, but it was in a frenzied attempt to violate, torture, and murder as many of Nanking's fearful citizens as they could in the shortest possible time rather than to protect them. The carnage went on for months. When they tired of their normal methods of mass murder, they held "killing contests" for sport. One soldier pitted against another tried to single-handedly kill more Chinese than his opponent in a specified period of time, usually an hour. The weapons of choice varied but swords were favored and the scores ranged into the hundreds of victims. Wagers were won and lost on who collected the highest body count. All-in-all somewhere between three hundred thousand and a half million Chinese lost their lives in and around Nanking. These deaths included countless innocent civilians and *"children of tender years."* According to reliable eyewitnesses, several of them foreign government officials, the Japanese behaved in a manner to rival, *"Attila and his Huns."*

Witnesses later gave first hand accounts of orgies of rape and murder. According to testimony at the Tokyo War Trials, *"Even girls of very tender years and very old women were raped in large numbers throughout the city, more than 20,000 during the first month of occupation alone. Many of these women were raped in public, then killed and mutilated and often left in stairways and streets for all to see."* Rev. James McCallum was in charge of the University of Nanking hospital at the time. His diary read, *"I know not where to begin or end. It is a story too horrible to relate. Rape! Rape! Rape!*

Never have I heard or even read of such brutality. We estimate that at least 1,000 rapes take place every night and as many more by day. A bayonet stab or bullet immediately greets the victim's slightest resistance or even a witness's disapproval. Horrible. Just horrible." Professor Hubert L. Sone of the Nanking Theological Seminary wrote, *"We thought with the coming of the Japanese soldiers, order would be restored, peace would return, and the people could go home and get back to normal life again. Surprise of horrible surprises! Robbery, looting, torture, murder and rape, burning; every atrocity that can be imagined was carried out from the very first moment and without limits or restraint. Modern times have witnessed nothing to surpass it. Nanking has become a living hell on earth. No person or thing is safe. Soldiers take anything they want, destroy what they don't want, and execute anyone who dares to object. Women and girls are raped openly, publicly and repeatedly by the scores and by the hundreds. Any who dare protest are shot or bayoneted on the spot and left bleeding on the cobbles. Even children who condemn the terrible mistreatment of their mothers and sisters are killed. One woman who was being raped had her four-months-old baby at her side. The baby cried out and the soldier, while continuing to rape the mother, smothered the baby to death with a pillow."*

Today in Japan, official policy about military brutality in China and elsewhere ranges somewhere between revisionism and denial. A look at Japanese history textbooks for middle and high school students reveals no mention of the *USS Panay* and almost nothing about the many crimes against humanity. There is almost no mention of the Sino-Japanese War at all. A short paragraph or two is all that tells young Japanese of their country's behavior in the 1930s and 40s. One textbook, Nihonshi B (Japanese History B) does make some slight mention of events. *"Japan sent in massive forces and occupied Nanking, the capitol of the Nationalist government. On that occasion Japanese troops killed many Chinese, including soldiers who had surrendered or been captured, and went on a rampage of looting, burning and raping."* The writer then goes on in a rather hurt tone; *"This was internationally censured as the Great Nanking Massacre."* The text then puts the number of total dead at a little over 100,000, a fraction of the actual count. Even this watered-down version of history finds little favor with school administrators in Japan and fewer than seven percent of high schools there use this text. Revisionist history is a danger facing many nations today. If we are ever to learn from our mistakes, we must portray things as they actually happened. To revise history in one's favor is to cheat future generations of any opportunity to do better.

The "Panay Incident" was Japan's first overt act against the United States and it went almost unnoticed. From The New York Times, August 31, 2000 - *Arthur F. Anders died Sunday at his home in Rancho Bernardo, Calif. He was ninety-six. Anders, nicknamed Tex, was a Navy lieutenant serving as executive officer aboard the USS Panay when it was attacked by Japanese warplanes in 1937.*

Tex Anders was born in Weimar, Texas in 1904. After graduating from the U.S. Naval Academy in 1927 he served on several vessels in Central American and Asian waters before the Panay Incident. His wife, Muriel Anders, died in 1990.

He is survived by his son, William Anders, Maj. Gen. USAF, Ret. of Deer Harbor, Wash.

Anyone who has followed the United States' Space Program will remember William Anders. He was an astronaut aboard Apollo 8 when it circled the moon in 1968.

The Panay Incident was an ominous event in the turbulent years preceding World War II. Japan had invaded China in July of 1937 and in November, Japanese troops besieged Nanking on the Yangtze River in east central China. Japan later apologized for the attack, which it blamed on poor visibility, and also offered to pay reparations.

After *Panay's* commanding officer was seriously wounded early in the raid and despite wounds of his own, Anders took command of the little ship. He issued instructions and kept what ordinance remained operational firing at the attackers. Later, when flying shrapnel tore through his throat rendering him temporarily speechless, Anders wrote his orders out on paper. For his actions that day Anders received the Navy Cross and a Purple Heart.

The little flotilla had been slowly making way up the Yangtze. In the lead was the shallow-draught river gunboat *USS. Panay*, one of five designed to patrol the Yangtze, show the American flag, and protect American interests before and during China's civil war. In *Panay's* wake lumbered three Standard Oil barges, two tiny British gunboats and several other smaller craft, all attempting to flee the Japanese under *Panay's* protection. The mood aboard was tense. Just the day before the flotilla had been fired upon from shore. *Panay* had been a target many times before, fired at by outlaw bands of Chinese guerrillas but never seriously damaged. Her captain, Navy Lieutenant Commander J.J. Hughes, was sure, however, that what had happened the day before was not the act of guerrillas but a deliberately planned and carried out attack led by rogue Japanese officers. In this estimate, he was correct.

For more than two miles the previous day, the little flotilla had passed under the guns of a shore battery commanded by a Japanese colonel named Hashimoto who had been a ringleader in the assassinations of Japanese government officials back home. Hashimoto ordered continuous fire on the *Panay* and her charges as long as his guns were able to bear. His likely objective, one shared by many radical officers, was to force the United States into a declaration of war against Japan. In his mind this would eliminate any interference from complacent civilians and military leaders left in the Japanese government. Fortunately for the flotilla, Hashimoto's aim was as erratic as his thinking and the firing was so wild that *Panay* and her flotilla, although making very slow headway against the mighty Yantze's current, passed safely out of range without being damaged. Time and luck, however, were about to run out for *Panay* and her charges.

More than three weeks before the fall of the city, with Japanese forces approaching Nanking, Chinese leader Chiang Kai-shek's foreign office notified the American Embassy that it must evacuate. Ambassador Grew, his staff, and most other personnel had departed aboard *USS Luzon* but a few civilians stuck it out until the last moment, then on 11 December they left aboard *Panay*. Next morning, 12 December, found *Panay*, three tankers and some smaller boats anchored midstream about twenty-seven miles upstream from Nanking, near Hoshien. American flags were flying from all of *Panay's* masts and Stars and Stripes were also painted brightly on her top and sides. It was a clear and deceptively peaceful Sunday morning, sunny and still with perfect visibility.

In spite of the tense mood, the crew savored their customary Sunday chicken dinner. They then secured for what they expected to be a peaceful afternoon. All guns were covered and unloaded. There was really no need for concern, the crew assured each other, because the United States was officially neutral in the conflict on shore. Unofficially many of the crew, like citizens back home, hoped to see the United States come into the war on the side of the outgunned and beleaguered Chinese. The arrogant behavior of the Japanese had degenerated into taunts and threats against all foreigners in China, military and civilian alike. The crew was also aware of the Japanese soldiers' bestial behavior as they had advanced on Nanking. Suddenly, at 1330 the peaceful day of rest was shattered as eighteen bombs fell, released by three Japanese Navy heavy bombers passing high overhead. The little ship's forward 3-inch gun, one of two, was instantly put out of action and the pilothouse, sick bay and boiler room were all badly damaged. The captain was seriously wounded, as were several crew and passengers.

In Anders own words: *"That Sunday on the Panay, we had just finished our chicken dinner. We heard Japanese heavy bombers coming. It wasn't a new sound. They were hitting the Chinese ashore, but the Japanese hadn't struck us because America was neutral in the conflict. This time the heavy bombers didn't wing past us and strike the Chinese on shore. The three heavies came right over us and unloaded. They were followed almost immediately by six low-flying dive bombers."*

Although wounded badly in the hands, Anders took over command of the bridge for his disabled captain. Shouting orders, he brought the *Panay's* machine guns to bear against the attacking Japanese planes, the second of the two more powerful 3-inch guns also being out of action by then. Twenty-one more Japanese planes attacked in the wake of the heavy bombers, twelve dive-bombers and nine Zero fighters. For the next thirty minutes or so they bombed and strafed the little ship repeatedly. After shrapnel tore through his throat, making speech impossible, the Navy officer grabbed a clipboard and gamely wrote orders out by hand.

Panay fought back as best she could with her .30 caliber machine guns but with very little effect. By a few minutes after 1400, all electrical power gone, engines cold, and deck awash, Anders wrote one last order; "Abandon Ship!" Lifeboats were lowered and all hands departed the sinking *Panay*. Japanese fighters continued to attempt to strafe the lifeboats as they made their way to shore. When the victims took refuge in heavy reeds that lined the swampy riverbank, Zeroes returned time and again trying to mow down the reed beds with machinegun fire and kill the hiding survivors. Luckily for the Americans, Japanese accuracy was again erratic. Accounts of casualties vary, but one or two bluejackets and one civilian, an Italian journalist, lost their lives and from fewer than a dozen to fifty persons, military and civilian, were wounded. Two of the three barges also went to the bottom of the Yangtze. Aided by friendly Chinese civilians, the survivors managed to get word through to Admiral Yarnell, Commander of the U.S. Navy's Asian Fleet. *USS Oahu* and the British ship *HMS Ladybird* picked the weary group up two days later.

Ambassador Grew, remembering America's outrage and nearly instant declaration of war against Spain for the sinking of the *Maine* in Havana harbor less than four decades earlier, fully expected the United

States to immediately declare war upon Japan over the sinking of the *Panay*. In this he was mistaken and had grossly underestimated two key elements of society at work at the time, one American, the other Japanese. Grew didn't realize just how powerful the "America First" isolationist movement had become in the United States with its mood of strict anti-involvement. He perhaps can be excused for this miscalculation, but as an Asian ambassador, he should have known that, unlike the arrogant Spaniards, the Japanese could be extremely conciliatory when it suited their purposes.

For several years before the sinking of *Panay*, Japanese extremists at home had been busily planning and carrying out assassination plots. They tried to cut down anyone who opposed their immediate goal of taking over most of Asia. The refusal of Japan's Finance Minister to further increase expenditures for the Army resulted in his summary execution by Army radicals. Also murdered were Admiral Saito, Lord Keeper of the Privy Seal and General Watanabe, the Inspector General. It was dangerous even to be related to those who were slow to cooperate with the extremists. An assassination attempt against Admiral Okada, the Prime Minister went awry when the killers mistakenly shot his brother-in-law instead. Alerted by the noise and commotion, the admiral escaped out a back door. The Genro, a group of elder statesmen that advised the Emperor, was then slowly but systematically infiltrated with "yes men" who were either loyal to or intimidated by military extremists. The average Japanese citizen considered their emperor a god, directly descended from the Sun Goddess. Of course, everyone knew that many bureaucrats advised the emperor and ran the government for him, but the man in the street believed the emperor to be all-powerful and as faultless as he was omnipotent. In actual fact it was the Genro who pulled every string of Japanese government, at the same time always being worshipful of and respectful to their divine emperor.

Emperor Hirohito was a sensitive, reclusive man who enjoyed more than anything his scientific experiments and collecting of marine biology specimens. As the military increased in power, he become more of a coddled prisoner than leader, manipulated with the gentlest of kid gloves and trotted out on display whenever required. It suited the purpose of Japanese warmongers to use the emperor but they knew the citizens would rise up in revolt if their emperor was not revered and treated worshipfully by his government "advisors."

The assassinations predictably sent waves of apprehension rippling throughout the Genro. They hurriedly met and selected a new cabinet to be led by a man they felt would satisfy the militants, a man who not only wanted a stronger military, but whose name was also quite similar to the emperor's, Hirota. As soon as Hirota finished meeting with his new cabinet on March 13, 1936, he made his intentions clear. His aim was to at once begin further military buildups, shifting commercial industry over to constructing a giant war machine with many more ships and airplanes. He also sent more "peace-keeping" troops to China while secretly preparing for war with that country. All that was needed now was a spark to ignite the situation. Hiroto, however, was still above all else a statesman and when the Army submitted yet another unrealistically inflated military budget, he balked and like anyone who didn't kowtow to the military, he had to go. His administration lasted only a short time. His successor, a General Hayashi, didn't satisfy the extremists either, and his régime endured for only a few days. In June, Prince Konoye came to power. The prince despised what was happening to his country, but he knew he didn't have the capacity to thwart the militarists and felt he could help Japan more from inside the government than from without.

For their part the Chinese were embroiled in a civil war and the Nationalist forces of Chiang Kai-sheck weren't anxious to provoke the foreign invasion forces. They had enough problems with these pesky Communists. They couldn't foresee that the Communists under Mao Tse-tung would ultimately win the war and take over China. Historians disagree over whether it was the Japanese, the Nationalists, or Mao himself who struck the first spark that ignited total Japanese aggression and led to all-out war in China, but they all agree the act suited his purposes very well.

Almost exactly four years after the fall of Nanking, Japanese planes were to once again drop their bombs and torpedoes on American shipping, this time at Pearl Harbor. In the aftermath of an attack that no amount of apology would ever erase from the minds of those who lived through it, a rallying cry brought the Americans together and forced them out of their apathy, "Remember Pearl Harbor!" This fervent cry drowned out any remaining protests from isolationists and other anti-war factions in the United States. Bombs and torpedoes rained from the sky in a clandestine attack the American President called, *"a date which will live in infamy."* Fortunately, for the Americans the attack missed the aircraft carriers and also failed to destroy vital fuel dumps and ship repair facilities, two fatal mistakes that were to later haunt the Japanese.

Investigations after Pearl Harbor showed that others had unwittingly provided the Japanese with a blueprint for the attack on Pearl Harbor. These included two Western fiction authors, one from England, the other from the United States, and Navy Admiral, H.E. Yarnell. He was the same admiral who would later investigate the sinking of the *Panay*. Several years before the *Panay* Incident, Yarnell himself showed the ever-observant Japanese the best way to attack Pearl Harbor. Japan then took these ideas, improved upon them and used them against the Americans.

Two novels were published during the early 1930s, outlining in detail fictitious Japanese sneak attacks on Pearl Harbor. An American author wrote "*Invasion America*", but "*The Great Pacific War,*" which came out of England was also very popular in the United States. Both books discussed in detail a Japanese surprise attack on the U.S. Fleet at Pearl Harbor, sinking most ships at anchor there and destroying nearly all shore-based planes. Fuel supplies and other infrastructures were destroyed, followed by similar attacks on Guam and the Philippines crippling American forces there. The English author, Hector C. Bywater, was naval correspondent to the London *Daily Telegraph*. His book received a favorable critique on the front page of the *New York Times Book Review* under the heading, "If War Comes to the Pacific." Both books immediately became study materials for senior officers at Japan's Naval War College. When the Japanese later attacked Pearl Harbor, their Supreme Commander of Naval Forces was Admiral Isoroku Yamamoto. At the time the English book was being reviewed in New York, Yamamoto was serving as naval attaché to the Japanese embassy in Washington. He was an insatiable reader and both books provided Yamamoto much food for thought which he surely memorized before passing on to his superiors.

In 1932, naval leaders in Japan as well as the United States were given even more to consider by U.S. Navy Admiral, H. E. Yarnell, future commander of the Navy's Asian Fleet and investigator of the *Panay Incident*. The purpose of a huge joint Army and Navy exercise held in Hawaiian waters that February was clearly outlined in its tasking messages. It was, "*to train the joint services in operations involving the defense of the Hawaiian Islands against attack. Specifically, it will serve to determine the effectiveness of an air, surface, and land attack against Hawaii as well as the adequacy of air, surface, sub-surface and land defenses there to repel such an attack.*"

Yarnell was commander of the attacking forces, comprised of the major portion of the Battle Force, United States Fleet. A fiery naval officer from the old school he was often described as being as peppery as he was "salty," no small compliment among sailing men. He was also known for not always playing strictly by the rulebook. He threw the book away again this time and not only did he catch the Hawaiian forces with their defenses down, he invented that most effective of modern naval war machines, the aircraft carrier attack force. By doing so, he also helped plant a very dangerous idea in the minds of Japan's naval leadership.

As the gigantic flotilla left California waters under Yarnell's command, battleships, cruisers and other ships plowed along in the traditional fleet convoy. Up to this time, the commander had always flown his flag from the largest battleship in the group. Yarnell however, was not only an unorthodox leader, but also an early staunch supporter of naval air power. On this exercise his flag flew from the masthead of the aircraft carrier *Saratoga*. Taking cover in a sudden squall, he broke away unobserved with just two carriers, *Saratoga* and *Lexington*, along with an escort of fast destroyers. His action ushered in the carrier task force concept, unknown at the time but soon to be eagerly adopted by the Japanese for later use against the Americans. War game defenders on Oahu were tracking the large, slow-moving fleet, preparing for a conventional assault, still days away as, approaching under the cover of darkness, Yarnell launched every aircraft he could get into the air. Just before dawn, 152 "enemy" planes thundered out of another rain squall, this one from northeast of Kahuku Point. The defenders were expecting some sort of limited air attack in a few days, but nothing of this magnitude, and certainly not this soon. Well hidden by the rain clouds over the Koolau Range, the planes, swooped down to wreak simulated havoc on the defending forces. All opposing aircraft were on the ground, still covered with camouflage nets. Yarnell had gained complete air supremacy and destroyed every objective. His carrier-launched raid came early on a sleepy Sunday morning, on the seventh.... of February, nearly ten years prior to the Japanese attack.

Like baseball games, war games must have umpires to keep score and render decisions. Ideally, no ships, planes or people are actually destroyed during these exercises, so it's up to the umpires to decide who wins or loses "the war." According to the umpires at Pearl Harbor that Sunday morning in 1932, Yarnell lost. In wargames, as in baseball, there are often some terrible calls. Although Yarnell had completely surprised and "destroyed" every objective, the Chief Umpire concluded: *"It is doubtful if air attacks can be successfully launched against Pearl Harbor in this manner. Strong defensive aviation forces would subject attacking carriers to the danger of material damage and the attacking air force to unacceptable losses."*

Why this didn't happen to Yarnell's forces, the Chief Umpire failed to explain, but there were just as many traditionalists in the U.S. Navy at the time as in Japan's military and it's very likely the task force attack was just too new and radical for the judges. The lesson was not lost on the Japanese, however and in 1936 the Japanese Navy War College brought forth a document entitled, *Study of Strategy and Tactics in Operations Against the United States.* This paper pointed out, *"In case the enemy's main fleet is berthed at Pearl Harbor, the idea should be to open hostilities by a surprise total attack from the air."*

The question that appeared on the final examination for every member of a graduating class from Japan's Naval Academy for a decade beginning in 1931 remained until shortly before the actual attack. Of the hundreds of suggestions, none approached the depth with which the two authors and one U.S. Navy admiral had pointed the way. Unfortunately for the Americans, only the Japanese were to heed the words and actions and see the potential to destroy the U.S. Navy Fleet at Pearl Harbor. In retrospect, many "dumb mistakes" concerning our lack of readiness in the Pacific have surfaced. The two books and the admiral's attack are among the least known but most devastating.

In the early fall of 1941, a Japanese ship arrived in Honolulu. Among those aboard were four men posing as stewards, but who were actually intelligence officers in the Imperial Japanese Navy. Two of these spies were air operations and surface ship experts, the other two submarine specialists. The ship had taken a far-northern route, passing close to the frozen Aleutian Islands. No suspicions were raised as the undetected ship busily plotted an exact course later to be followed by the Japanese carrier task force that attacked Oahu. Planners of the assault also faithfully followed the suggestions of the writers and the admiral and they had digested these lessons well. Japanese military officials were now testing a proposed route to be followed later by the attacking fleet. To their satisfaction the ship bearing the four naval experts met neither ships nor aircraft on the desolate sea route to Pearl via the Aleutians.

The four "stewards" took ample shore leave during their stay in Hawaii, admiring all the usual tourist sights, especially the military installations. They were very curious, taking plenty of pictures and talking with locals, both Japanese and Hawaiian. They even took tourist plane rides over Pearl Harbor, snapping many more photos from the air. They were testing a plan which so far looked to be an excellent one. The Japanese Consulate in Honolulu supplied the four men with maps of Pearl Harbor and surrounding military airfields. The spies also purchased many postcards with views of Pearl Harbor, Battleship Row and the mooring sites at Ford Island and the Naval Base.

Returning home, they presented a confident report to their superiors. Pearl Harbor was both extremely approachable and vulnerable. The plan was a good one, spies and leaders agreed. It was the strategy used on another sleepy Sunday morning, December 7, 1941. Following the same route as the earlier ship, Japanese carriers launched hundreds of planes and in less than two hours, eight gigantic battleships, three cruisers and several other ships had been sunk or severely damaged. One hundred and eighty-eight planes were destroyed and 2,400 men killed at a cost of fewer than thirty Japanese planes, no ships and very few men lost.

This marked the beginning of a very long and dangerous road for America's fighting forces. It would be years before we were to come home again, and many of us didn't make it.

That Most Infamous Day

December 7, 1941

I was up early on that balmy Sunday morning. Just turned nineteen and promoted to Private First Class, I was feeling pretty good about things in general but that was about to change in a matter of minutes. Sunday was normally a day of rest and relaxation for those of us not on duty. Most Marines who weren't out on liberty liked to "sack in," then catch chow at the mess hall just before it closed for the morning.

I had big plans for later on and I didn't want to be late. I was going to take my first flying lesson. I had already had my breakfast and, dressed in utilities, I was taking it easy on my bunk, shooting the breeze with a couple of buddies until time to leave. Utilities are a Marine's work uniform normally prescribed by the commander as "uniform of the day." We wore them for all informal duties. I planned to change into khakis, a light tan tropical uniform, before leaving for my appointment. This dress uniform was required to exit the Naval Base gate, I would then walk the short distance to the civilian airfield and begin flying that day if at all possible. I had always wanted to fly and was very anxious to get started.

Our barracks was typical for the 1940s. Many of them dated back to long before the First World War and weren't always in the best of shape. Two floors with open bays were filled with double-tiered bunks and not much else. Latrine areas featured open lavatories and urinals, gang showers, and elbow-to-elbow sinks and mirrors. At the foot of each bunk, stood a footlocker about five feet long with several removable compartments that held most of our worldly possessions. Under each top bunk, attached to the frame, rested our rifles slung by cords. We considered our Model 1903 .30-06 caliber Springfields our best friends and took very good care of them. Manufactured before WWI, the Springfield was an extremely accurate 5-shot, bolt action firearm.

I didn't get to go flying that morning but I did see more airplanes than I could have imagined. Hundreds of fighters, dive-bombers, and torpedo planes passed over Pearl Harbor and other nearby targets. My Springfield rifle was soon ripped free of its cords and placed into action. The first major American action of World War Two was about to begin and I would be right in the middle of things.

My buddies were just lazing the morning away, dressed only in their GI boxer shorts, called skivvies, which we always slept in. Still with sleep in their eyes, they were idly shooting the breeze. I had just returned from breakfast and was killing some time before going to sign up for my lessons. I really was happy for the chance to learn to fly but I didn't get my opportunity that day.

Since mine was a bottom bunk and near the window, it was a favorite place to sit. My friends were camped out on it because it was quite warm and the morning breeze felt good. Open bay barracks have no chairs so you either sat on your footlocker or bunk, or stood. Suddenly we heard the sound of several explosions coming from the direction of the harbor. The noise was muffled and we couldn't really identify it but we thought it might be an exercise or more dynamite detonations. The engineers had been blasting in the harbor earlier in the week. Either way we figured it didn't concern us but as things turned out, it sure did.

Drawn by the sounds we went over to the window for a better view. The next instant, a plane flew by, level with us and just a few feet away. It was so close it seemed like I could reach out and touch the wingtip or throw a stone into the cockpit. Two Japanese airmen looked over at us and we looked back at them. They smiled at us but it wasn't a very friendly smile. My buddies grabbed for their clothes while I snatched my rifle, empty cartridge belt and steel helmet. I rushed down the stairs and ran next door to draw some ammo from the armory.

As I hustled to the administration building that housed the armory on the lower floor, Japanese planes were passing overhead in growing numbers, heading in several directions at different altitudes. At the armory I met up with an immovable object, a corporal who had his instructions and planned to follow them to the letter. *"No ammunition without the proper written requisition slip,"* he told me. Then he folded his arms across his chest and glared at me with a look that plainly said no PFC was about to change his mind. Luckily a burly sergeant rushed in and overheard the corporal's comments. *"Break out the ammo!"* he shouted. The corporal reached under the counter and pulled out the only bandoleer of rifle ammo he had open. *"Sergeant, that's all I've got,"* he said. *"Well, let's get some more broken out,"* replied the sergeant and as they rushed into the storage room and began breaking cases open, I hurried out onto the parade field. Just as I was coming out, my buddies showed up, but they had to wait a few minutes for the ammo. I raced out onto the parade field, pulled a full clip from the bandoleer and inserted it. Just then, a Japanese plane thundered low over the barracks and across my line of fire. I got one shot off at it before it was gone. Several other planes flew over at low altitudes and I soon emptied my clip. As I was reloading, my buddies and some more Marines rushed out onto the parade field and began firing with me. My two friends dropped down beside me and one of them tossed me a full bandoleer. I flipped it over my shoulder and we set up a steady firing.

The parade field in front of the Marine barracks. Marines waiting for the second Japanese attack.

Japanese fighter plane

Soon runners were bringing us more ammo and as they gave us fresh bandoleers we continued to fire at planes passing overhead. Japanese aircraft were everywhere, flying in both directions. Some flew very low over our parade field and the warehouses as they came from the piers and ships in the harbor. Others flew higher over us and on to Hickham Army Airfield near the naval base to drop bombs there. I also got off one shot or sometimes two at these planes.

The Marines of the 3rd Defense Battalion had only recently returned to Hawaii after being relieved at Midway Island. The Battalion, numbering nearly nine hundred officers and men had garrisoned Midway for seven months, since 27 January 1941. The 3rd had first arrived at Pearl Harbor 7 May 1940, after a month-long cruise aboard the USS Chaumont, from the East Coast to the West Coast and then on across the Pacific. This was part of a move by the Chief of Naval Operations to build up defenses in the Pacific to counter anticipated possible Japanese aggression. The bulk of the battalion remained at Pearl for eight months of training. Small reconnaissance details, followed by larger advance parties, did preliminary work supplying and installing initial defense installations on Midway. Later the entire battalion, nearly one thousand strong, moved to the island.

Detachments of the 1st Defense Battalion were deployed to Johnston Island and Palmyra. The 6th Defense Battalion was moved from San Diego, where it had been training, to Pearl to take the 3rd Battalion's place there and stand by for further orders. The 6th would later send men to Midway and also serve as a reserve unit supplying replacements to the other battalions, as required.

The 14th Naval District, headquartered at Pearl, was responsible for administering and providing personnel for several Pacific islands. Their policy when possible was regular rotation of the men from these outlying posts back to Hawaii, replacing those that had been longest "in the field" first. This was necessary because time spent on these islands was a tough mix of hot work and crushing boredom.

In midsummer a group of 1st Defense Battalion personnel was deployed to Midway to begin the relief of the 3rd Defense. On 11 September the 6th Defense Battalion returned to Hawaii for a well-deserved break from several months of work on the defenses at Midway. Little did anyone suspect that three months later the monotony on the island would be interrupted by an enemy attack.

After returning to Pearl the Third began a routine of days spent cleaning, repairing and inspecting equipment. Weeknights were spent in the field on training maneuvers but many weekends were reserved for liberty. Unless scheduled for guard duty, a man could "hit the beach," the term for going to town. That's where most of them were on December 7th and only two or three dozen of us fell out that morning. We remembered our rifle training well and of the twenty-nine Japanese planes shot down, the Navy later credited us with three confirmed kills with just our rifle fire.

Japanese airplane wing taken from a plane shot down by Marines. The wing was detached and moved to the barracks. The pilot had nine holes in him.

One of the three planes crashed nearby, skidded across a tennis court and collided with a base-housing unit. After the attack, some men got into a truck and drove over to take a look. They came back to report that we had put nine rounds into the pilot. The men also took one of the wings off and brought it back with them to put in front of our barracks. We all cut off a little piece of the rising sun for a souvenir.

There were nearly 100 ships anchored at the U.S. Naval Base and along the Ford Island piers across the harbor that day. My barracks faced the harbor and piers but sat behind some warehouses across the drill field, which obstructed our view.

We were caught completely off guard but that didn't prevent countless acts of individual heroism. I will mention just two stories. One is of a commissioned Navy officer on the *USS Arizona*, senior among the survivors and chosen to receive the Medal of Honor. Another was an African-American sailor serving as a messman on the *USS West Virginia*, whose story is one of the best known.

Aboard *USS Arizona* at 0755 hours, 7 December 1941, Lieutenant Commander Samuel G. Fuqua had already enjoyed his breakfast. Up early, he had on a dress white uniform because he was planning to attend church services on the fantail at 0800 hours, but they would not convene that morning. Instead, there would later be many memorial services for the sailors, Marines and other personnel killed in the attack.

Sam Fuqua was Damage Control Officer on the *Arizona*. As soon as he heard the air raid sirens he called the bridge to learn what was happening. No drill was scheduled, and there was no answer from the bridge so he headed topside thinking that perhaps an unannounced exercise might have been called without his knowledge. He knew that Rear Admiral Isaac Campbell Kidd, commander of Battleship Division I, was aboard.

Kidd was proud of all his battleships but *Arizona*, the largest, was his favorite. Captain Franklin Van Valkenburg was also proud of commanding *Arizona* and considered her "his ship." It was just possible the two had called a surprise air raid drill thought Fuqua, but the damage control officer should certainly have been alerted. On the bridge the two senior officers could not believe their eyes. It was easy during the first moments of the raid to believe some sort of drill was underway, rather than an attack from a nation some 4,000 miles distant who had not even declared war. Many first mistook the attackers for friendly aircraft and even as bombs hit it didn't immediately register what was happening. Then American planes parked on the runways at Ford Island began exploding in balls of fire. Mushrooms of flame erupted from the decks of *Utah* and *Raleigh* at the northwest side of Ford Island, and flaming oil began pouring from the ruptured sides of *Oklahoma* and *West Virginia* on Battleship Row as all doubts vanished.

The admiral and the captain quickly took charge while screaming Val dive-bombers passed over their deck, some only 20 feet above it. As the projectiles struck, *Arizona* began to tremble with the impact. Sailors frantically manned their guns and tried to bring them into action but the ammunition was securely stowed below deck. Then the *Arizona* rocked violently and Fuqua was thrown to the deck, temporarily losing consciousness. Regaining his senses, he found himself beside a gaping hole in the ship's deck. Debris lay everywhere, the sky was black with smoke and cries of the injured and dying surrounded him. Finally he heard the sound of some return fire as a few big guns opened up. He picked himself up and continued towards the bridge where his two superiors were valiantly trying to save ship and crew. He could see wounded sailors emerging everywhere, many of them blinded by the blasts. In pain and amid chaos, men were running for the railings, intent on plunging into the sea below. Some of their comrades attempted to restrain them, knocking several unconscious to keep them from leaping into the pool of liquid fire below.

All around, the sea burned with a searing heat as fuel oil blazed up the sides of the ship and the steel plating became too hot to touch. More enemy planes roared in and one armor-piercing bomb penetrated the deck near the bridge, struck the forward powder magazine and exploded. It acted as a detonator for a million and a half pounds of high explosives. The bridge vaporized and killed all hands stationed there including the captain and the admiral. The *Arizona* broke in half and began to sink.

Commander Fuqua quickly assumed command and issued the order to abandon ship. He then personally forced dazed and injured seamen to seek the safety of lifeboats or jump. Moving through the flames that burned all around him he rounded up the few straggling survivors on deck and herded them to safety. He refused to give in to the fires and explosions that were consuming his ship until he had reached and rescued all he could. Finally, he boarded a boat and headed away from the sinking ship. Even then he didn't seek safety but compelled men on the little boat to help him search the water for more survivors.

Lieutenant Commander Samuel Glenn Fuqua received the Medal of Honor for his heroic actions that day. Born 15 October 1899 in Laddonia, Missouri he retired as a Rear Admiral and passed away on January 27, 1987. He is buried in Section 59 of Arlington National Cemetery.

Doris Miller was born in Willow Grove, Texas on October 12 1919. He was the third of four sons born to Connery and Henrietta Miller. The family was far from well to do and used the services of a local midwife for the birth rather than a hospital. It was common practice in those days for midwives to predict the sex of an unborn child. This particular midwife had a very good record and she had promised the Millers a daughter. She was wrong, but how she or the parents decided to call the new baby boy "Doris" is a mystery. In all likelihood she had already helped them pick the name. Midwives back then often claimed occult powers to go along with their birthing skills and most families bowed to their wishes.

From Willow Grove School, "Dorie" went on to W.L. Moore High School in Waco. He was a stout young man and enjoyed playing football. It was the era of the "Great Depression" and he also worked as a cook in a small Waco restaurant to help supplement his family's meager income. He tried to join the U.S. Army, then the Civilian Conservation Corps. The CCC was a Depression-era government program that offered small wages, a bed and meals to young men in exchange for heavy labor building roads, clearing timber, etc. In both attempts he failed, probably because of his skin color. Dorie was just a month shy of his twentieth birthday when he entered the U.S. Navy at a Dallas recruiting station.

After completing boot camp at Norfolk, Va., he was assigned to the *USS West Virginia* as a messman, one of few jobs open to African-Americans and other minority sailors in the pre-war Navy. His work was similar to that of a butler or batboy. He attended the ship's officers while they ate in their dining room, called the mess, and helped maintain their quarters and uniforms. These menial jobs were delegated primarily to blacks and Filipinos who were recruited directly from the Philippines. Both races were restricted until 1948 from holding more desirable jobs in the services. In that year, President Harry S. Truman, signed a bill aimed at desegregating the armed services, but it was many more years before the bill obtained the desired results. A closely related rating, or job specialty, to messman was steward. In less than two years, Miller rose to Mess Attendant Second Class. A second class petty officer was the fifth rung up the enlisted rate structure and Miller's promotion was quite rapid advancement in those days.

On December 7, 1941 Mess Attendant Second Class Doris Miller was sorting laundry just before 8:00 a.m. when the first Japanese bombs began falling. The *West Virginia* was at anchor, as were all battleships in Pearl Harbor. As bombs began blasting his ship, Miller rushed to the main deck where he helped carry his mortally wounded commanding officer to shelter. Leaving his C.O.'s side, he then rushed out on deck. He was ordered to pass ammunition to two men trying to fire an unmanned antiaircraft gun but they were as inexperienced as Miller. The officer who gave the order soon noticed that Miller was the one firing away at the attacking planes, while the other two men loaded for him. This was his first experience firing such a weapon and it is amazing that he was even able to put the gun into action, let alone bring it to bear effectively. Black sailors serving in the segregated Navy were not given any training on firing ships' guns.

Just how effective his firing was that day is open to question. News stories credited him with downing from two to five aircraft, a somewhat unlikely number. Survivors of the action say the smoke was so thick on the *West Virginia* that it was almost impossible to see. Miller himself later told Navy officials that he might or may not have hit anything. The number of planes shot down aside, the remarkable fact was that he was able to handle the gun at all and continued firing at the enemy until ordered to abandon ship.

For his actions that day, Dorie Miller was awarded the Navy Cross. He was given Christmas leave in 1942 and went home to Waco to visit his family. It was the last time they would see their son. After his leave, he reported for duty to the aircraft carrier *U.S.S. Liscome Bay* as a mess attendant, first class. On November 24, 1943 the *Liscome Bay* was torpedoed during the battle of the Gilbert Islands. This time Dorie Miller didn't make it off the sinking ship.

On military bases, most significant buildings bear the names of notable military persons. The Navy named a dining hall for Doris Miller, then a barracks and finally a ship, the destroyer escort *USS Miller*. In Waco, the YMCA building, a park and a cemetery are named in his honor. In Pennsylvania and Texas, elementary schools proudly bear his name. In Los Angeles, there's a Doris Miller post for Veterans of Foreign Wars and in Austin a college auditorium is named for him. In Chicago, the Doris Miller Foundation honors persons who make significant contributions to racial understanding. Dorie Miller helped pave the way for black and Filipino sailors and is still making a positive impact on the lives of citizens today nearly sixty years after he gave his life for his country.

Pearl Harbor was a superbly planned and executed sneak attack, but several major blunders and errors in judgement were to haunt the Japanese and lead in great part to their final downfall. They failed to destroy the Americans' fuel supplies and ship repair facilities. The *U.S.S. Pennsylvania*, which was in dry dock at the time, was hardly scratched. Another mistake was leaving the "tank farms," storage for the petroleum, oil and lubricants, called "P.O.L," untouched. I was sent over to help protect the tank farm after the attack.

Two other factors were to also help deny the Japanese their dreams of a "Greater Co-prosperity Sphere." All American aircraft carriers were safely at sea that morning and would later prove a major force in the Pacific war. Another, perhaps greater factor was what Admiral Yamamoto referred to when he was appraised of the complete success of the sneak attack. *"We have awakened a sleeping tiger,"* he said. Occidentals have been trying for centuries to unravel even the surface workings of the "inscrutable" Asian mind. Yamamoto's thinking seems at times confused, even contradictory to us.

He had attended college in the United States and saw duty as naval attaché at the Japanese embassy in Washington. His education and stateside experience should have told him that the Americans would retaliate in force after the sneak attack. He also wrongly assumed Americans would be totally demoralized by the destruction at Pearl Harbor and shortly sue for peace. In this, the normally brilliant military strategist had completely misjudged America's will to fight. Angry Americans would be very slow to forgive the Japanese and many have not done so to this day.

The mighty American war machine immediately began gearing up and was soon unleashing its power against not only the Japanese in Asia, but their German and Italian allies in Europe as well. British Prime Minister Winston Churchill was quietly jubilant over the sneak attack. While always showing a sympathetic face to Roosevelt and the American people over Pearl Harbor, he privately said he could have hugged the Japanese for bringing the Americans into the war on England's side at her "darkest hour."

After the second wave of Japanese warplanes left Oahu, we were taking a much-needed break and watching the smoke rise from ships at Ford Island and the harbor. A truck pulled up and a Corporal called out, *"Hey you two!"* pointing to me and another man, *"Get in the back of the truck!"*

All along the docks and piers, men were making their way ashore swimming or clinging to debris. Small boats brought in wounded from "Battleship Row" across the harbor at Ford Island. The battleships had been hit hard and *USS Arizona* and most of her crew lay on the bottom. By the time we arrived, rows of burned and badly wounded men were lined up, waiting for first aid and transportation. Our truck made its way down to the docks where injured men were lying, unable to walk the short distance to the base hospital. We loaded as many as possible and headed for the hospital, trying to be as gentle as possible. There were so many wounded that they overflowed the hospital corridors and

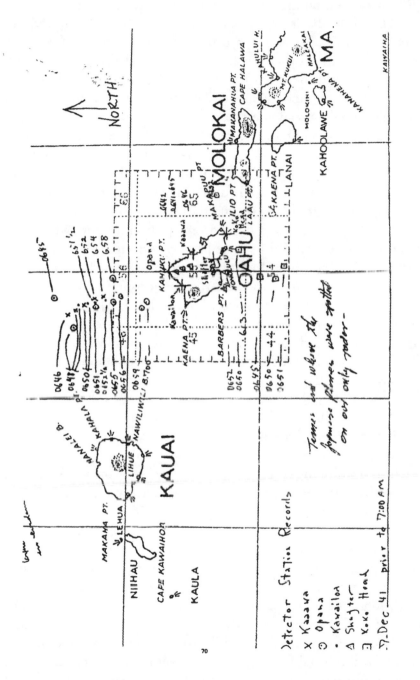

Radar sightings of Japanese fighter planes

spilled out onto the grounds and we were forced to lay ours on the grass. We made several more trips before we were relieved.

When I got back to the barracks late in the day, I found my name posted on the bulletin board ordering me to report for guard duty. Soon I was in another truck, this time headed out to the tank farm. Everybody out there was nervous, not knowing whether or not the Japanese might attack by land or launch more air attacks. For all we knew, they could already be ashore. A few nervous sentries fired at shadows during the night and there were fires on the nearby hillsides and in the sugar cane fields. We didn't know who set the fires but we were all worried about them. There was no action, however, and soon everybody settled down and walked their posts in silence.

I had rushed to make my guard duty assignment and brought nothing to eat or drink. I was alone on my post and I got awfully dry and hungry. The second day I spotted a jeep coming my way and was I ever thankful when they filled my empty canteen. The driver also gave me a can of something to eat. After the jeep left I looked inside and found it contained hardtack from World War I. My dad probably ate some just like this, I thought. It was as hard as a rock but soaked in a little water it was delicious, at least to a starving Marine.

I was finally relieved on the second afternoon and returned to the barracks where I got cleaned up, found something to eat, and collapsed into my bunk. I slept like a dead man until it was my turn for guard duty again. For the next week we were all either sleeping, eating, or somewhere marching a post or guarding something. The entire battalion was sent out to defend against a possible attack, which we all felt sure would be coming soon. At the end of the week a friend told me to check the bulletin board and my name was on there again, this time ordering me to get ready for immediate deployment. The notice didn't mention to where.

Many of us who were pulling guard duty didn't sleep or eat for at least thirty-six hours after the attack. The more fortunate were able to make their way to the mess halls where mess cooks had returned from fighting to begin preparing meals and dispensing them around-the-clock to all comers, including civilian ship workers. Many thousands of meals were supplied and the emergency food service continued until normal feeding locations were back in action.

Misinformation and fear were our greatest enemies in the first hours after the attack. Unconfirmed reports circulated that drinking water had been poisoned, more bombings had occurred and even that amphibious landings were occurring at various points on the island. Each Marine had his gas mask close at hand because commanders considered the threat of gas attacks a very real possibility. After all, someone capable of a sneak attack would think nothing of using gas against us, they reasoned.

Two incidents should have tipped off authorities of the pending raids. First was the sighting by two Army privates of a "large flight of inbound unidentified aircraft" on a brand-new radar station at the Oahu coast. Radar was such a recent development that when the technician called the sighting in, his officer-in-charge didn't heed the warning. The installation was so new that it didn't even yet have a communications link to headquarters. The operator had to walk to a gas station pay phone to call in. He was sure of his sighting, however, and insisted that his OIC check into it. A flight of some dozen B-17 American bombers was due in from the states that morning. That, the operator was informed, was what was on his radar screen. He was then ordered to secure the radar set and return to base. Before doing that, the two Army privates who had begun tracking the approaching aircraft at 0645 hours continued plotting them all the way into Pearl Harbor, taking a reading every minute or two.

A second occurrence was even more extraordinary, a yet-to-be explained blunder. More than an hour before the Japanese planes arrived, the American destroyer, *USS Ward* spotted, reported and sank a small two-man Japanese submarine near the mouth of the harbor, killing one crew member and capturing the other.

A heavy anti-submarine net was normally stretched across and protected the mouth of Pearl Harbor. It was to be opened only to let American ships enter or leave the harbor, then promptly closed again. Its purpose was to protect the vulnerable ships at dockside from possible submarine attack. The net had been opened in the early hours of December 7th, and for some unexplained reason remained unclosed for several hours afterward. Recent research points out the possibility that more than one of the five Japanese midget submarines entered and launched torpedoes that day and the attack on Pearl Harbor was actually a combined air and subsurface sea assault.

At least two Japanese mini-subs slipped into Pearl Harbor that morning. The *Ward* sank one with depth charges and gunfire and another was rammed and depth-charged the destroyer *Monaghan* after the raid began. A third midget sub had the bad luck to run upon a reef just outside the entrance channel to the harbor. This sub was fired upon by yet another destroyer, the *Helm*. Although severely damaged it managed to slip away and eventually washed up on the other side of the island near Bellows Field, a small auxiliary air station. Weakened from inhaling fumes, one of the two-man crew died before reaching shore. The other was later captured, sound asleep on the beach, completely exhausted and dispirited.

When the flight of B-17s did arrive at Oahu later that morning, they found themselves surrounded by Japanese planes. Flying in from the States, the big bombers were low on fuel and totally unarmed. They were immediately attacked by "Zero" fighters and then, as they approached closer, confused American gunners fired on them as well. The big planes scattered to attempt landings at any spot they could find to put down. One shot-up bomber, unable to make it to a landing field, put one of Oahu's many beautiful golf courses to a new use as a bomber landing field.

Most of the 3rd Defense Battalion was held on Oahu to provide security and to stand ready to meet an expected Japanese invasion force. The anticipated attack never arrived but I would not know one way or the other because I had embarked for places unknown. I hardly had time to clean up, eat, and pack my gear before leaving the Hawaiian Islands.

My name was on the bulletin board again, this time along with about two dozen other Marines from the 3rd Defense. We were all that could be spared from the battalion's many duties in the days after the attack. We formed a small part of a relief convoy ordered to join a larger task force proceeding to reinforce Wake Island against the Japanese. Our convoy failed in its primary goal of relieving Wake, not because of lack of trying but because the Japanese had already overrun the island before we were even well underway.

I wound up on another island I had never heard of and would spend the next few months there waiting for the Japanese to attack.

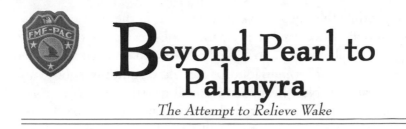

Beyond Pearl to Palmyra

The Attempt to Relieve Wake

After the attack on Pearl Harbor, we spent a nervous week pulling guard duty and preparing defenses. We were all expecting an invasion or at the least another air assault and all sorts of crazy rumors were flying including one that all drinking water on the island had been poisoned. Coming in from guard duty one night I heard that my name was listed on the board to leave Hawaii. The notice contained about twenty-five names and directed us to get packed and ready to depart. Where we were headed I didn't have a clue but there was some speculation among others whose names were on the list that we might be going to try and relieve the men at Wake Island. I didn't join in on the discussion, but instead packed my gear and stood by.

Around midnight a couple of trucks pulled up in front of the barracks and we loaded into them along with our weapons and gear. After a short, dark ride we jumped down onto a pier and were hustled up the gangplank of a destroyer. It was pitch dark with no moon and no light was visible anywhere because of the blackout conditions. We boarded in complete darkness thinking the Japanese planes could return at any time. We were urged to board quickly and had no sooner hastened up the gangplank then we were ordered below decks where we found our bunks and spent a nervous night. It was 15 December, one week after the attack.

The destroyer was the *U.S.S. Thornton*, an old, post-WWI era "four-stacker," each funnel pouring forth billows of black smoke whenever extra power was called for. The *Thornton*'s keel was laid in 1919 and she had seen little action, but this was about to change. Enemy eyes were already watching from submarines prowling below the surface. The Japanese submarines, part of a force of twenty-nine that had been in the area since before the attack, were lying in wait for any ships leaving Pearl. *Thornton* was part of what I soon learned was a sizable convoy bent on rushing the 4th Defense Battalion and any other men who could be spared to help defend Wake Island.

Next morning after breakfast we all made our way up topside for some fresh air. It was a beautiful, sunny morning and we were looking forward to spending the day on deck, resting up from the exertions of the past week. We soon discovered that Japanese subs had plans that would intrude upon our relaxation period. We had been up on deck for only a few minutes when the *Thornton's* loudspeaker blared out, right above my head. "Now hear this! Now hear this! General quarters. All hands man your battle stations!" We could contribute nothing to a sea battle and were expected to get out of the way and let the Sailors do their jobs of defending the ship. Our duty station for general quarters was our bunk area and I rushed down the ladder, ears still ringing from the loudspeaker and waited with the others. We weren't able to tell what was going on but we knew the destroyer was dropping a pattern of depth charges because we could feel the vibrations running right through the ship. We later learned that there were at least two submarines and probably more attacking us. One of them was sunk by one of the other destroyers and the rest were driven off.

A few days later we were in the thick of trouble again, and were ordered to be deathly quiet. It was pitch dark and of course the entire convoy was running at "darken ship" with all outside lights secured and only dim red light inside the tightly closed hatches. This time they told us why we had to be so quiet. We were right in the middle of a huge Japanese battle convoy. They couldn't see us because it was so dark but they could pick up even the slightest sound with their sonar and other listening devices. There wasn't a sound to be heard on any of our ships.

After the sneak attack on Pearl Harbor, President Roosevelt addressed the American people and told them to be prepared for the loss or capture of several American bases in the Pacific, one of which was Wake Island but planners decided to send a relief convoy to try and save Wake. While ships were still smoldering in the harbor, they were already putting their heads together but many problems lay ahead. Much of the U.S. Fleet was at the harbor bottom and many ships were permanently out of commission or damaged beyond any immediate use. Wake, like the other outer islands would have to stand or fall on its own unless helped by the meager resources being put together at Pearl.

Total Marine forces on Oahu in December 1941 were made up primarily of the 3rd and 4th Defense Battalions, both at full their strengths of about one thousand officers and men apiece. The two battalions, along with elements of the 1st Defense Battalion, and other barracks and shipboard Marines totaled fewer than 3,000 men. Relief for Wake would have to come from these units at the expense of other vital needs on Oahu.

Planners chose the 4th Defense Battalion to relieve Wake, with a bit of help from the 3rd and a few more Marines taken from other Hawaii-based units.

Defense battalion quartermasters had a very limited supply of war material when the fighting broke out, but radar sets and fighter aircraft were already on their way to Wake from San Diego via Pearl Harbor aboard the carrier *U.S.S. Saratoga*. The aircraft were primarily from Marine fighter squadron VMF-21. According to her log, *"Sarah"* and other ships had departed California waters at a convoy speed of eight knots on 8 December, one day after the attack at Pearl. On 9 December, Admiral Kimmel's staff began planning to send a relief task force to Wake as soon as *Saratoga* arrived, even at the expense of protecting Hawaii. The task force was to be built around *Saratoga* and consisted of three cruisers of Cruiser Div. 6, nine destroyers of Destroyer Squadron 4, the seaplane tender *Tangier*, and fleet oiler *Neches*, among others. These ships, packed with what troops and equipment could be spared, made up Task Force 14, of which I was part. While TF-14 sailed for Wake, another task force, built around the carrier that brought me to Pearl, *U.S.S. Lexington*, was ordered to make a feinting strike 800 miles south of Wake in an attempt to draw the Japanese away from Wake and toward the vicinity of Jaluit. This was Task Force 11. A third task force built around another carrier, *U.S.S. Enterprise* commanded by Vice Admiral "Bull" Halsey, had orders to conduct operations in support of the relief effort from just to the west of Johnston Island.

The 4th Defense Battalion was chosen to be the prime Marine relief force because of its readiness. The Fourth Defense had recently been deployed from Guantanamo Bay, Cuba. Quietly they had boarded a transport ship in late October 1941 and made their way through the Panama Canal. This was about the same time the 3rd Defense was returning to Pearl from Midway. Six weeks later they arrived at Pearl Harbor on Monday, 1 December, a week before the attack.

On 7 December, men of the 4th Defense manned a 3-inch gun battery at the Navy Yard a short distance from where a couple dozen or so men and myself brought down three planes with our Model 1903 rifles. They also served on several anti-aircraft fire teams. It was because the 4th had just completed an overseas movement that it's men and equipment were thought most ready for immediate service, while my outfit was still getting our equipment ready after those months of deployment on Midway. The 4th was the logical choice to relieve Wake with only a few of us from the 3rd sent along to help.

On 10 December, the 4th was alerted for immediate deployment. The destination was not given but many of the men thought it would be Wake. Nightfall found them busy trying to square away their equipment in pitch darkness. They groped blindly in blackout conditions to assemble personal gear in time for loading. In the midst of all this frantic activity came confusing orders to knock off and return to their original positions. CinCPac, Commander-in-Chief Pacific, wanted to make another study of the entire situation before sending such a large relief force to Wake because it might desperately be needed in Hawaii or elsewhere.

There was some grumbling among the men but the task force couldn't leave without *Saratoga* anyway and she was still at sea doing her eight knots and would not arrive in Hawaiian waters for several more days anyway. Two days later, CinCPac issued a final decision. The mission to reinforce Wake Island was "a go" and we would sail as soon as *Saratoga* arrived and refueled. The carrier finally arrived during the night of the 14th, but could not enter the harbor to refuel because of the submarine nets. The Navy now refused to open them at night for any reason, fearing a submarine attack. It was the next day before "*Sara*" entered Pearl Harbor to begin loading operations. Some mistakes about refueling at sea would later prevent the relief force from reaching Wake on time and we all wound up at other locations.

Several units of the 4th began embarking on 12 December. I had been busy pulling guard duty and knew nothing of plans for me until my name appeared on the bulletin board and we departed.

The defenders on Wake had earlier made their most pressing needs known to CinCPac. A list of critical provisions was forwarded to Pearl Harbor where supply activities did their best to fill it. These items were sent down to Pier 10 at the Navy Yard where they were logged and loaded aboard the seaplane tender *USS Tangier,* a ship whose job was to supply and repair the Navy's big "flying boats." Ship's inventory listed two radar sets, the SCR-270 early-warning radar and SCR-268 fire control radar set. Ammunition stores included 9,000 rounds of 5-inch ammo, 12,000 3-inch shells with 30-second timed fuses, and three million belted rounds for .50 and .30 caliber machine guns. Also included were large stores of grenades, small arms ammo, anti-personnel mines barbed wire for stringing perimeters, and engineering tools. All of these materials were critical to Wake's defense as was additional equipment and tools intended to help the defenders repair their already bomb-damaged weapons and supplies. Included were three complete fire control and data transmission systems for 3-inch batteries, replacement equipment for the atoll's 5-inch guns, electrical cable, ordinance tools and other provisions and spare parts. Among the units of the 4th Defense were 3-inch gun Battery F, 5-inch gun battery B and a provisional machine gun detachment drawn from Batteries H and I. A headquarters section was also drawn from the Fourth's Headquarters and Service Battery.

Initial command of the relief force was given to First Lieutenant Robert D. Heinl, Jr. as it finally formed up to await embarkation on 13 December, but his command was only an administrative appointment lasting less than two days. Prior to departure command passed to Colonel H.S. Fassett on 15 December. Fassett was under orders appointing him island commander once he reached Wake, orders he would never be able to obey. After loading, *Tangier* moved to the upper harbor where Rear Admiral Fletcher's Cruiser Division 6 was waiting for Saratoga. The carrier entered the harbor on the 15th and as soon as refueling and loading was completed the entire task force set course for Wake. Once at sea we were told our destination was Wake Island, but almost as soon as we were given that information, the mission was canceled and we were told the Japs had already landed and taken all survivors prisoner. We all felt awful when we heard that.

Marines were almost never told their destination until at sea. This was to prevent the enemy from gaining information about ship and troop movements. Where we were going didn't matter too much to us anyway and when we heard of Wake's fall, we knew it meant only that we would land to fight somewhere else. On the ships' bridges, however, there was bitter cursing and even weeping at being ordered to abandon the mission. As one destroyer captain put it, *"The crying and cursing near me grew more and more mutinous in its tone. I couldn't bring myself to order the men to belay their talk so I silently left the bridge, for I felt exactly the same way myself."*

Our convoy split up into three groups, part headed to Johnston Island and another group to Midway while our ship was sent to Palmyra along with another ship, the *USS Sumner*, which carried our gear. When we reached the place we found a number of small islands in the shape of a big horseshoe. Eight of us were assigned to one small island where we set up our tents, dug foxholes, strung barbed wire and built an observation tower. The engineers and their bulldozers later connected most of Palmyra's islands but ours remained separated by a stretch of shallow water.

On one of my first nights on guard duty, I was up in the tower scanning the sea around us when suddenly I saw a bright object in the sky that looked like a second moon. It was so large I thought it might be a secret weapon or something and immediately phoned the Command Post and reported my sighting. The CP told me to relax, it was the just the evening star. I wasn't used to the way stars looked in the black sky above a Pacific island. They were huge.

Years before the attack on Pearl Harbor, the importance of several Pacific atolls had been recognized, Palmyra among them. According to a plan received at Pearl Harbor the day after the sneak attack, the duty of the fleet would now be a defensive holding action until losses at Pearl could be replaced. The Navy's mission was to support the Army in protecting the Hawaiian Islands, Wake, Johnston, Midway, Palmyra and others. Now that Wake had fallen, our convoy was split up to do just that.

The idea of using outlying Pacific islands to protect Hawaii and other United States interests including the mainland from Japanese attack was not new. Palmyra, along with Wake, Johnston and Midway were selected in 1938 to serve as an outer defense perimeter for the Pacific Fleet's homeport at Pearl. Each was selected because it was capable of hosting one or more airfields. The Navy started its outer base development scheme in late 1938, following the plan for expanding them presented by the Hepburn Board, a Congressionally authorized fact-finding group. In the spring of that year, the board had made a study showing that a critical need existed for these bases.

Midway, Wake, Johnston and Palmyra had great potential value according to the group's findings. Under the long title of, "Report on the Need for Additional Naval Bases to Defend the Coast of the United States, its Territories and Possessions," the document recommended immediate preliminary action. Surveys were quickly conducted at each location, followed by plans to begin in 1939 and 1940 with the construction of several bases, airfields and seaplane facilities, called seadromes.

The Pearl Harbor raid found none of these islands completed or even near ready to perform their missions. All were scheduled to have Marine garrisons, a requirement not yet filled in most cases. Guam, in the Japanese-controlled Marianas, did have a small Marine Barracks detachment whose fate was sealed early as it was sadly written off in all war plans and its early capture by the Japanese conceded. The rest of the islands were placed in a category that called for Marine and other defense forces sufficient to repel major attacks. Sadly most of the work was still to be accomplished and most forces were not yet in place. A modified plan was quickly drawn up to meet as many of these requirements as possible.

The responsibility for developing garrisoning plans and situating the coastal and anti-aircraft gun positions was given to Colonel Harry K. Pickett, who wore two hats, 14th Naval District Marine Commanding Officer and Commanding Officer, Marine Barracks, Pearl Harbor Navy Yard. Colonel Pickett had personally surveyed most of the proposed base sites long before the attack and now gave his best effort on their behalf. He promised active cooperation from Pearl Harbor on requests for men and material to complete the garrisoning plans. This is why my ship was diverted to Palmyra after the landing at Wake failed. It also explains why some jobs were handed us for which we had never been trained. There was a plan and it would be followed one way or another to combat this emergency situation.

Palmyra was a classical Pacific atoll, as were Johnston, Midway and Wake, each consisting of several rather bare, low-lying sand islands within a coral reef. Each atoll had just what the planners were looking for. At least one island at each location was large enough for an airstrip and lagoons within the reefs were sufficient, sometimes after dredging and blasting, for seaplane landing and taxiing lanes and ship anchorages. Midway and Wake were also designated for development as forward bases for the fleet's submarines. Civilian contractors were called upon to build the installations, but until war actually broke out, the men who would defend them, Marines of the Defense Battalions, did most of the work on the island defenses.

Palmyra and Johnston were physically small and their living areas so limited that it was impossible to put more than a small detachment on each island. When we arrived at Palmyra, a lot of bulldozing and dredging was going on connecting some islands and deepening approaches. The *Thornton* was able to find a channel deep enough to make its way right up to a dock to unload us. Palmyra consisted of dozens of little islands, most too small for habitation. A sergeant, along with six other Marines and myself were assigned to Bird Island. The reason for the island's name became immediately clear, especially to anyone who wasn't careful where they stepped. There were birds everywhere, millions of them.

We were ordered to build and man an observation tower. We also had a large searchlight and power plant to use in case an attacking ship or submarine needed to be "lit up" at night. I was power plant operator, which meant I was to keep up the generator that powered the light and tower equipment. I received extra pay for this, six dollars per month. This when added my base pay totaled a whopping thirty-seven dollars a month. Of course, we weren't receiving any pay at all because Marines in combat areas didn't get paid until rotated back for leave or a little R&R. The idea was that we didn't need money in the field and would only lose it or gamble it away. A combat tour of eighteen months usually earned a man R&R and he then received at least partial back pay. An extra duty for a power plant operator was to carry the Browning Automatic Rifle and the extra pay for this was another eight dollars per month. No BAR's were available on Palmyra however, so I didn't get this allowance. I didn't get my BAR until after landing on Guadalcanal.

Bird Island, with us and countless birds of every description, rested almost exactly in a horseshoe's arch. It was home to birds of all sizes and descriptions. Thousands of tiny shore birds ran in and out of the surf and did their best to avoid the much larger birds such as men-of-war and frigate birds. We were never without feathered company and the loud noise could drown out all human conversation when the birds were even slightly disturbed. They were everywhere and made their presence known from before sunrise until after dark by darting around our heads.

Coral bridges had been constructed to connect most of the islands but Bird Island was separated from the main island by a long stretch of seawater, two or three feet deep at low tide. A man could then wade over to the main island to get rations and ammunition. We used a small boat when the water was too deep and sometimes a boat or truck would deliver larger equipment, some of it totally unexpected.

A large sturdy tent up a trail from the observation tower and hidden out of sight from the water provided shelter. Our equipment included the searchlight, field phones and a radio and our job was to search for the enemy both from the tower and by patrolling along the shoreline. A sentry's job is normally the loneliest duty in the military but we often kept each other company since there wasn't much else to do. When not on duty, we had little to do other than sleep, eat and clean our equipment. Every night those who were off-duty would gather at the base of the tower, singing songs and passing time together. Anyone hearing us would have believed we were a very pious group because the only songs we all knew were the hymns we had learned as children.

One day I noticed one guy in the tent busily at work over a math book. Curious, I asked where he had gotten it and his answer would change my life. He told me he was enrolled in a special educational program just for Marines in the field. I looked on the back of the book, got the address and wrote off to the U.S. Marine Corps Institute, Washington D.C. Soon I had a math book of my own to work in and I was on my way to making up much of the education I had missed out on as a youngster. The program was through International Correspondence Schools in Scranton, Pennsylvania. I took a lot of courses and passed them all with good grades. I guess I had matured a little bit since my earlier days at school.

None of us had been trained to fire any of the larger weapons such as the 3" and 5" guns, but the Marine Corps had been issued a salvaged 3" piece from one of the Navy's disabled ships. They decided to install it on Bird Island whether anybody there was qualified to fire it or not. One day a truck arrived from the main island bringing us the 3" anti-aircraft gun. There was no doubt they wanted us to use it because they also sent along several cases of 3" shells. We got busy right away digging and dynamiting a pit-like gun emplacement in which we mounted the gun. Now it was time to fire the thing but no volunteers stepped forward until finally one of the men came up with a bright idea. We loaded the gun, tied a line to its trigger and got as far back down in our foxholes as possible. We didn't know if the thing would fire, misfire or maybe just blow up. Bang! It fired just fine so we left it sitting there and got back to our routine, not knowing what else to do with it. It wasn't too long before a Jap submarine surfaced near Bird Island and began firing at the airfield, still under construction over on the main island. This is what we had been waiting for. We fired back at the sub but I don't think we hit it. Our gun made a lot of noise though and got their attention and before long the sub went away. We decided maybe we had scared it off with all our loud, inaccurate shooting and congratulated each other.

I spent nearly six months on Bird Island but not much happened except for a lot of patrolling and staying ready and the one submarine incident. We watched the horizon for sight of a Japanese invasion fleet, which never showed up. When I was off duty I worked hard on my correspondence courses, learning many of the things I had missed in school.

One night while on duty, something appeared on the horizon that was never explained although it was seen and reported by nearly every guard post. I was sweeping the sea with binoculars looking for Jap ships and on one pass a huge, glowing red ball appeared on the horizon. It looked just like a big ball of burning fire. It was present for only a short while, then gone. I hesitated to report in because of my earlier star incident, but this was too amazing to let pass and I finally got on the field phone and called it in but I should have just kept this sighting to myself. I found out later that nearly all of the men on guard duty had reported the same thing, but we all got a typical response. *"Does it look like a Jap ship to you? It doesn't? Well what are you supposed to be lookin' for over there? Quit tyin' up the lines with chitchat!"* We never saw the big red object again.

Sometimes we went swimming in the lagoon. I got hold of a pair of goggles and, wearing old sneakers to protect my feet from sharp coral and sea urchins, went diving along the reef looking for interesting shells. A favorite was called a "cat's eye," which after being left for a while to be cleaned up by the ants and fly larvae gave up a nice little gem-like half-moon disk from its center.

Bird Island also had many coconut crabs, bigger than a lobster, with one large, powerful claw that they put to good use shucking the layers of husk right off of coconuts, then cracking them open. You didn't get anywhere near that claw because you could lose a finger in a split second. In our spare time we hunted these crabs and soon had a nice little "cottage industry" going with the Navy. After we dispatched them with a pointed stick, we hung them up in a tree where big flies that inhabited the island could easily find them. In a short time the maggots had done their work and the shells were fairly clean. Then we scrubbed them in the surf and polished them up with sand. Now we were ready for business and when a ship came in we traded the crab shells to the sailors for whatever we could get, especially things we didn't have. The shells were unique, pretty and made great souvenirs.

We each had a ration of two warm beers per day, available over on the main island. We hardly ever made it over there and since each man had to pick up his own ration we couldn't send our boat for everybody's issue. It was just too much trouble for a couple of hot beers that nobody liked that much anyway. We preferred to make our own refreshments, using the pure grain alcohol we had in five-gallon containers for cleaning purposes. I don't remember the exact formula for our bootleg beverage because I have never been much of a drinker and didn't have any interest in it. I recall something about raisins and yeast from the mess hall and the men complaining it needed ice, something of which we had none.

For some, the blending of long hours with being away from home proved to be just too much to take. One day we spotted a man trying to leave in a rowboat, battling the surf and rowing hard to break clear of the reef. We climbed up into the tower to watch and could faintly hear his shouts but were unable to make out what was bothering him. Before long a big boat headed out from the pier and picked him up. We later found out that he was out of his head and ranting about going home. We then heard he had been drinking after-shave lotion. Not all the casualties in the Pacific came from Jap bullets. Fevers, sickness and mental fatigue were often our worst enemies. Some guys were just desperately homesick and two hot cans of beer per day didn't help ease that yearning. For our part we stayed to ourselves and kept busy working, polishing our crab shells, and having an occasional sip of homemade hooch.

One afternoon while I was on duty, a party of officers came trudging up the beach. They had come over from the main island and imagine my surprise when one of them turned out to be none other than Admiral Chester Nimitz, big boss of all operations in our area. He asked us how it was going and if we needed anything. He complemented us on our Navy gun and then left to visit other islands.

One night in the tower, I was tuning the radio to try and pick up some music. We often got broadcasts from a gal called "Tokyo Rose," a Japanese-American who was working for the Japs. She put out a lot of crazy propaganda but she also played good stateside music, so we listened to the music and ignored the chatter. Rose was our only music source until one night I came across another station, this one faint and scratchy, coming from a long way off. The host's name was Beverly and her show was called "Reveille with Beverly." I listened to her every chance I got after that and made a vow that if I ever got back to California where her show originated, I would go see her. A few battles later, I did just that.

About six months after arriving on Palmyra, we found another important bulletin on the board. The unit was being relieved and heading back to Pearl Harbor for R&R and to rejoin our battalion, but not me. My name wasn't on the list, I was told, because I had not been with the 3rd long enough to be eligible for rotation. Before I had joined the outfit they had spent several months on Midway and then rotated back to Pearl for R&R where I linked up with them. The Japanese had interrupted their R&R and they still rated a rest. They were all being sent back now for guard duty at Pearl but I would get to spend some more time on Palmyra. I was told to move my gear over to the main island where I would be assigned to the Fleet Marine Force and was to report to the headquarters building every day.

After about two months of this, I was told to report to the headquarters building where a sergeant asked me if it was true that I was a water engineer. "I am," I said and the sergeant told me to get ready to leave right away. Midway Island had a water problem, he said, and they didn't have anybody qualified to work on their distilling plant. A plane soon picked me up and after a quick stop at Johnston Island, I flew on to Midway. I didn't know it at the time, but this was the last I would ever see of Palmyra and I was headed for my first real battle of the war.

The Battle of Midway

How a Water Plant Fools the Enemy

After a short stop at Johnston Island, we landed on Midway, an atoll consisting of two main islands, Sand and Eastern. I had been sent to repair the Grissom-Russel water distillation unit on Sand Island. When I checked in, I was told to try and fix the system although they didn't seem too hopeful that much could be done for it and after a quick inspection I saw why. It looked like a horse somebody had ridden hard and put up wet. It was plain to see that no preventive maintenance had ever been pulled on it and the unit was in desperate need of cleaning and lubrication and badly clogged with calcium deposits.

I spent a full day cleaning, lubing and thermocracking the unit, a process of heating and cooling the pipes rapidly to crack calcium deposits. I rinsed out the deposits and before long had the unit running like a top. Everyone was grateful, if a little surprised. I don't believe mine was the only water plant on Midway. I was never told but judging by how hard it had been worked, and how happy they were to have it going again, I figured it must have been the only one on Sand Island and a big part of the fresh water supply.

Water was scarce on Midway, as on most of the islands and the loss of a distillation unit was felt up the chain of command. I was assigned to water duty full time and no mention was ever made of returning me to Palmyra. This suited me fine since my friends of the 3rd Defense weren't there any more. I spent every day pulling maintenance on my water plant and filling a large canvas tank with fresh water. From this tank I then topped off portable trailer-mounted tanks which were then towed to the various locations. Jeeps pulled the smaller trailers while heavier trucks hauled the larger ones. Whatever the trailer size, the drivers told me how welcome the water was.

I knew nothing of a distinguished visitor who arrived at Midway later the same day I came in, but I had already met the man on Palmyra. I didn't know about the information Midway's commanders received that day and I was also unaware that I would soon be called upon to operate another weapon for which I had received no training.

On 2 May Marine and Navy leaders on Midway got their first news that their island could soon come under Japanese attack. A plane landed and Navy Admiral Chester W. Nimitz, CinCPac stepped off. He had traveled personally to see the two senior officers on Midway, Lieutenant Colonel Harold D. Shannon, who was in charge of the 6th Defense Battalion Marines, and the atoll overall commander, Cdr. Cyril T. Simard. Midway was likely soon to be the site of a vast allied defense effort and Nimitz wanted to make sure Shannon and Simard were on top of things.

The admiral inspected all installations, then directed Shannon to submit a detailed list of what supplies and equipment he would need to defend against a strong Japanese force. Nimitz promised that all requested items that were available would be immediately provided. In less than a week men and material were being sent from Hawaii to beef up Midway's defenses.

Upon his return to Pearl Harbor, Nimitz arranged "spot" promotions for both Simard and Shannon. The naval officer was raised to captain and the Marine to colonel, their ranks remaining equal. Nimitz sent a joint personal letter of congratulations to the promotees in which he outlined the steps being taken to help reinforce Midway against attack. Japanese D-Day, predicted the admiral, would come on or about 28 May.

Midway was only one of several possible Japanese targets that Nimitz had to worry about but he urged the officers to prepare as if Midway was the only one. After reading the letter and congratulating each other on their promotions, Shannon and Simard spent several hours conferring on their final plans for defense. That evening, Colonel Shannon assembled his key personnel and advised them of a possible enemy attack. He then outlined additional defensive measures and priorities for final pre-battle efforts. All recreational and off-duty activities were suspended and May 25th was set as the absolute deadline for completion of all ordered defensive measures.

While at Midway, I was still attached to the Fleet Marine Force and not only out of touch with my unit but also not in contact with my parents or anyone else back in the States. My mailing address was FMF, Territory of Hawaii, but I didn't send or receive any mail during this period for two reasons. First, I didn't know where I would be or for how long what with all my moving around. Second, my records were missing, so FMF didn't know exactly where I was either. I was assured I would get a brand-new service record to replace the one that had been lost between Palmyra and Midway but so far nothing had been done. What I did get was an anti-aircraft machine gun. I didn't know about the Admiral's visit, but I felt something big was about to happen and I was right.

One morning a truck drove up and stopped near the water plant. The sergeant driver told me a large Japanese force could attack any time. He then issued me a .50 cal. machine gun and told me to shoot down any enemy planes I saw once I heard the air raid siren. There was a PFC with the sergeant who got out and stayed with me to help fire the gun. I was glad for the company and I could use the help. We got busy filling sandbags and built ourselves a fine machine gun emplacement. One thing there was no shortage of was sand to fill the bags. We got the gun set up and camouflaged, then spent the next few days filling more bags and piling them high to protect the plant. Then I kept to my routine and we waited.

The Marines on both islands completed their preparations by the May 25th deadline and on that day the commanders received two unexpected gifts. First was a coded message from Nimitz in which he passed the word via his staff that the Japanese attack was now not expected until early June. On the heels of this ten-day grace period arrived something even more welcome, reinforcements.

The *USS St. Louis* pulled up to Midway's docks on the morning of the 25th. On board was a 37mm anti-aircraft battery consisting of eight guns on loan from my old unit, the 3rd Defense back on Hawaii. Also aboard were two very welcome rifle companies of the 2nd Marine Raider Battalion. Four of the new guns came to Sand Island, along with Raider Company C, commanded by Captain Donald H. Hastie. Raider Company D, under 1st Lieutenant John Apergis and the other four guns were set up on Eastern Island.

On the 26th, *USS Kitty Hawk*, an aircraft tender, arrived with 3rd Defense Battalion's 3-inch Anti-aircraft Group commanded by Major Chandler W. Johnson. Also aboard was a light tank platoon of five tanks. For Marine Air Group 22, which was still flying antiquated fighters known as Brewster Buffaloes and outmoded Vought Vindicator dive-bombers, there was a special treat. Kitty Hawk brought for MAG-22 sixteen SBD-2 dive-bombers and seven comparatively new Grumman F4F-3 fighters plus extra pilots. The following week additional Army and Navy aircraft arrived until, by May 31st, Eastern Island had 107 aircraft. There were twenty-one Army bombers, four B-26s and seventeen B-17s, twenty-two Navy seaplanes, sixteen PBY-5As and six TBFs and sixty-four Marine Corps aircraft, nineteen SBD-2s, seventeen SB2U-3s, twenty-one F2A-3s and seven F4F-3s. The daily usage of aviation fuel, known as AVGAS, was about 65,000 gallons.

Ground forces and civilian workers who had remained behind to help defend the island were as busy as their military counterparts. Reinforcing weapons were installed, tanks tested for travel in the sand, gun emplacements checked, a large system of obstacles and mines put down, and demolitions finished. Our island was completely encircled with two double-apron barbed wire barriers and all installations on both islands were ringed by protective wire. Homemade anti-boat mines of sealed sewer pipe and obstacles of reinforced steel were laid offshore. The beaches were strewn with homemade mines constructed of ammunition boxes filled with dynamite and twenty penny nails and cigar-box antitank mines covered likely beach landing locations. Hundreds of homemade bombs made of bottles filled with gasoline, plugged with a rag fuse and called Molotov cocktails stood ready.

A decoy airplane was "mocked-up" from plywood and other scrap materials to draw enemy fire. It was dubbed the "JFU," (Japanese fouler-upper) and sat prominently on the seaplane apron. All underground fuel storage areas on Sand Island were prepared for emergency destruction in case the islands fell.

The fuel demolition system worked a little too well when a sailor threw the wrong switch blowing up a good portion of the aviation fuel stores. The AVGAS supply was so critical after this costly mistake that the pilots who arrived on the *Kitty Hawk* got no chance to check out in their SBD-2's prior to going into battle. The blast also destroyed pipelines and MAG-22 ground crews had to refuel all planes after that using hand-pumps connected to 55-gallon drums, a very strenuous and time-consuming operation.

By the first of June, everything was as ready as possible to stand off a major assault and we would not have long to wait. Forces at work on both sides would make Midway the first major engagement of the war where we were on a more equal footing with the Japanese. Unknown to me, my water plant, or rather its history of problems, would play a major role in the American carriers and support ships being at the correct spot to fight the Japanese. As unlikely as it might seem, Midway's water supply problems would prove to be a dominant factor in the enemy's downfall.

When Midway's water plant went down a mild panic followed until I arrived and got it running again. Message traffic was hot and heavy between the local commander and CinCPac staff. Without the distillation equipment, water would have to come from another source, either flown in or brought by ship. Ships visiting Midway had no water to spare. Most ships are unable to distill water unless underway and even then have a tough time making enough for their own use. It was this message traffic, intercepted by chance on Palmyra, that alerted a sergeant there who remembered that I had been to water engineering school. Luck was to play a major role in the Battle of Midway and the failure of the island's water purification equipment was what set the stage for the entire engagement.

Naval code breakers had busted the Japanese "Purple" code weeks before, but this often proved less of an advantage than might be supposed. The Japanese wrapped many of their messages in secret phrases, cryptic meanings, and codes-within-codes. Sometimes with especially sensitive subjects this was intentional but it was also part of Japanese culture. The first thing many people comment on when discussing the Japanese is their hidden meanings and this carried over to their message traffic as well.

Nimitz had a problem. He felt fairly sure that Midway would be the enemy's next target but he had to be sure. To commit the fleet to Midway and have the Japanese strike elsewhere would result in another disaster like Wake. The solution to this problem lay in his subconscious and concerned, of all things, my little water plant.

Admiral Spruance makes a strong case for luck in battle. One piece of luck made sure American ships were in place to do battle with the Japanese fleet and it was my water plant that, without my knowledge, played a key role. Otherwise the American fleet might have been thousands of miles from Midway, guessing which island the Japanese would strike. I knew nothing about this, of course. I just made as much fresh water as I could every day and kept my canvas tank full, ready to fill water trailers. I was amused in the movie; "Midway" when Midway's radio operator said he had just been over to the water plant and it was working fine. Neither my helper nor I ever saw anybody near the plant except the truck drivers as they pulled up with their water trailers.

The message was sent out and received by both American and Japanese radio stations. The next day Yamamoto sent the fateful message that was to cost him four carriers and nearly all of Japan's best flyers. His message was in code and was quickly decoded by the Americans. It read in part, "AF is experiencing severe fresh water problems."

The pleasure of Nimitz' staff can be imagined when they were able to rush to their commander with the good news. *"Sir! It's Midway!"* Nimitz hurried to issue orders directing his carrier commanders to proceed at all speed. He had, with the counsel of his senior advisors nearly made the decision to commit most of his resources to Midway's defense but it was important to be sure. Another incident at Midway three months earlier helped him make his decision. This one was in the air.

On 10 March, while construction work and reorganization was going on, Marine flyers got a chance to test their planes against an enemy aircraft when Midway's radar picked up an unidentified blip about forty-five miles west of the atoll. The target was a four-engine Japanese "Mavis," a Kawanishi 97 flying boat. Twelve fighters under Captain Robert M. Haynes rose and were vectored out to intercept it. They attacked and although the flying boat made a good account of itself, shot it down.

This contact was more important to Nimitz' staff as intelligence than the Marine pilots could know. Two such aircraft had tumbled four bombs into the hills just missing Honolulu a week earlier on the night of 3-4 March and this led Nimitz to believe that the attack might mean a second Japanese offensive against Hawaii.

The Marine's air action near Midway gave added strength to his opinion that Midway was the intended target. After CinCPac intelligence added other factors brought to them via the broken Japanese codes most felt sure the next strike would be against Midway. If it fell, Hawaii would surely be at the top of the Japanese list of near future targets. The water message convinced everyone that Midway would be hit soon.

Nimitz ordered a major fleet sortie to a position 300 miles northeast of Midway from which a Japanese offensive could be intercepted and fought off. The admiral put all his chips on Midway and won. He put Rear Admiral F. J. Fletcher in command of Task Force 17, which included the *Yorktown*, two cruisers and six destroyers. *Yorktown* had just limped into port from the Battle of the Coral Sea and engineers estimated it would take ninety days to put her back into fighting shape. Following a harsh order from Nimitz they had her in near-fighting condition in two days.

Fletcher was under a bit of a cloud because of his command decisions at the loss of Wake. Some Naval leaders openly questioned his decision to refuel his relief force at a crucial point allowing the Japanese time to attack and take Wake. Nimitz placed command of Halsey's two carriers, *Enterprise* and *Hornet* under a new commander because Halsey had a minor illness. "Bull" had just rushed his carriers and Task Force 16 back from a run nearly to the Coral Sea to launch Lt. Col. Jimmy Doolittle's sixteen B-25s for a first strike against the Japanese mainland. Halsey was in sick bay and Nimitz followed his recommendation to use Spruance to command the task force. It was an interesting decision because Rear Admiral Raymond A. Spruance had plenty of experience in cruisers and lighter ships, but no time commanding carrier forces. Nimitz gave overall tactical command to Fletcher, who was senior to Spruance.

While Nimitz readied and deployed his floating forces, the Japanese completed their Midway assault plans and polished off the rough edges with carrier training and bombing rehearsals. By the end of May, all Imperial Fleet attack units were underway. On the decks Japanese sailors, still riding the high of Pearl Harbor, sang victory songs, sunbathed and relaxed. The Pacific was their oyster and they were suffering from something called, "The Victory Disease," a false sense of security that ran through every level of planning for the Midway offensive. American flyers, those waiting on Midway and those steaming toward their date with the Japanese Fleet, were about to offer a sure cure for the "disease." First though, those of us stationed on the ground at Midway would have to receive our baptism of fire, courtesy of the enemy flyers.

A Navy PBY, flying patrol from Midway was first to spot the approaching Japanese ships at about 0900 on 3 June. The seaplane tracked the enemy long enough to report that they were making about nineteen knots eastward headed straight for Midway. These vessels were probably the transports and seaplane groups of the Japanese "Occupation Force." Captain Simard sent out nine B-17 bombers that searched much of the day then made contact and attacked at 1624 hours. The pilots reported having hit "two battleships or heavy cruisers" and two transports in a large group that was then only 570 miles from Midway. The excited flyers were wrong on both counts that afternoon. They attacked fleet oilers not battleships and they scored no hits. A Catalina flying boat did launch a torpedo into one of these oilers later that night in a moonlight run.

This action convinced Fletcher that the battle would soon be on and he changed course from his station 300 miles east-northeast of Midway to a new position about 200 miles due north. From here he felt he could launch his planes the following morning against the Japanese carrier forces which were expected to come in from the northwest. U.S. intelligence was still good, thanks to the broken Japanese codes. Vice Admiral Chuichi Nagumo, acting under Yamamoto's watchful eye, was steaming for Midway with four of Japan's largest fleet carriers *Akagi*, *Kaga*, *Hiryu*, and *Soryu*. His orders were to launch against Midway, soften it up for the invasion forces, then steam on to intercept and destroy the remaining U.S. Pacific fleet if it challenged from Pearl Harbor.

Even as his transports and oilers were under attack, Nagumo continued to steam in from the northwest. Near daybreak on 4 June, as *Yorktown* launched an early morning search mission and eleven PBY's were rising from Midway to patrol for the enemy, he reached a position about 250 miles northwest of his target. From this position, at 0430, the Japanese admiral launched thirty-six "Val" bombers along with an equal number of escorting Zero fighters for the first strike against Midway.

Meanwhile Midway's Marines were bracing for the first shock wave of Japanese planes. General quarters sounded and ground force personnel manned every available weapon. My helper and I jumped into our pit, I aimed the machine gun skyward and we watched the skies and we didn't have long to wait. MAG-22, which already had fighters up to cover the PBYs, was ready to launch their remaining planes. At 0555, shortly after a second PBY report fixed the position of the Japanese *Striking Force*, 6th Defense Battalion's radar picked up "many planes," as Naval Air Station radar reported the same blips.

Air raid sirens began to wail, Condition One was set, and all remaining MAG-22 pilots manned their planes. Both squadrons were in the air within ten minutes, VMF-221 headed out to intercept the enemy planes and VMSB-241 flew to a point twenty miles east, where the dive-bomber pilots would await further instructions. My helper and I double-checked our gun and sandbags and got ready.

VMF flyers under Major Floyd B. Parks sighted the zero-escorted Val dive bombers at 0616 about thirty miles out, and Captain John F. Carey, leading one of Parks' divisions flying in an F4F-3, launched a first strike against the enemy from 17,000 feet. The Marine flyers were hopelessly outnumbered, and reported that the Japanese Zero fighters could, "fly rings around us." They had time for only one pass at the bombers, and then had to turn their full attention to the swarming Zeros. Each Marine found himself with from one to five Japanese fighters on his tail. Of the dozen American planes in this brawl, only three survived. The damage they inflicted on the enemy has never been accurately given but they downed several bombers and some of the Zeros. Other Zeros chasing the American planes back over Midway were shot down by ground antiaircraft fire.

Another group of thirteen Marine fighters under Captain Kirk Armistead also came in to attack the Japanese air formation. Again the damage inflicted upon the enemy remains undetermined but this time fewer Marine planes were lost. The fighter protection of Midway had been used up and the job now passed to we defenders on the ground and our antiaircraft fire.

The first Japanese formation, twenty-four horizontal dive-bombers, attacked at about 0630 from 14,000 feet. Anti-aircraft fire knocked down two before they could drop their loads but the remaining twenty-two came on through the fire to unload their bombs on our positions. As these first explosions rocked us, eighteen planes of the second wave came over for their strike. Since each of these formations left their carriers with thirty-six planes, we had already knocked down more than half the enemy's strike force.

The attackers from *Kaga* were assigned to hit the patrol seaplane facilities on Sand Island where I sat behind my machine gun. They dropped at least nine 242-kilogram or 500-pound bombs, setting hangars ablaze and lighting off the fuel tanks 500 yards to the north. The *Akagi* planes plastered the north shore of Eastern Island, destroying our mess hall, galley, and Post Exchange. Japanese pilots returning to their carriers identified these buildings as hangars.

Other Japanese dive-bombers struck the already burning fuel dump at the north end of our island, our dispensary and Eastern Island's powerhouse, two direct hits by 805-kilogram bombs completely destroying it. Almost the last bomb of the strike struck the 6th Defense Battalion's command post on Eastern Island. The direct hit killed the Marine sector commander, Major William W. Benson and wounded several other men, most of them seriously. After these bombers completed their runs, the remaining escort Zeros came in on strafing runs. The first and only air strike on Midway Island was over just after 0700 hours.

Admiral Spruance realized the importance of the battle. In the introduction to his book, *"Battle That Doomed Japan"* he writes, "In reading the account of what happened on 4 June, I am more than ever impressed with the part that good or bad fortune often plays in tactical engagements. Authors gave us credit where none was due for being able to choose the exact time for our attack on the Japanese carriers, when they were at the greatest disadvantage - flight decks full of aircraft, fueled, armed and ready to go. All that I can claim credit for myself is a very keen sense of the urgent need for surprise and a strong desire to hit the enemy carriers with our full strength as early as we could reach them."

Before the American planes, both land and carrier based, had their go at the Japanese, we were called upon to defend ourselves against the heavy Japanese attack. The land-based planes hit the Japanese *"Striking Force"* in the morning, but with little success. Later, as Nagumo juggled planes and decisions throughout midday, the American carriers steamed southeast for an afternoon attack against the enemy.

Spruance had planned to hold his planes on their flight decks until he drew within about 100 miles of the Japanese, but when he heard of the air strike against Midway, he decided to take a calculated risk. The admiral ordered the launch of his carrier planes two hours before the originally scheduled launch point was reached. By this calculated gamble he hoped to catch the Japanese planes back aboard their carriers, rearming for a second go against the atoll. About twenty minutes later, Nagumo made the decision Spruance had hoped for and set his forces up as exactly the target Spruance prayed his pilots would find.

Enterprise and *Hornet* began launching at 0700, sending up nearly every operational plane aboard, except for a very few held back to fly protective cover for the task force. Leading the strike were twenty-nine Devastator (TBD-1) torpedo bombers. Sixty-seven Dauntless dive-bombers and twenty Wildcat fighters quickly followed while eighteen other Wildcats patrolled overhead and another eighteen stood by to relieve them.

Fletcher held his aircraft on *Yorktown's* deck for nearly two more hours. He thought these planes might be needed against any enemy carriers not yet located. He made the decision at 0830, with no other enemy carriers sighted, to launch half his dive-bombers and all of his torpedo planes, along with a heavy escort of fighters. By just after 0900, *Yorktown* had seventeen SBDs, twelve TBDs and six F4F-3s in the air, and all its other planes ready to launch.

Spruance hoped that Nagumo would continue to steam toward Midway and deployed his planes accordingly. Nagumo obliged by doing so for more than another hour until the first U.S. planes found the Japanese *Carrier Striking Force*. The flattops were in the center of a large force containing two battleships, two cruisers and eleven destroyers. Nagumo had recovered his Midway planes by 0917 and immediately executed a ninety degree change of course to east-north-east. This abrupt course change caused thirty-five of *Hornet's* SBDs and their escorting fighters to completely miss the battle, but *Hornet's* fifteen torpedo planes found the enemy fleet and initiated a low-level torpedo run with no fighter cover.

The obsolete Devastators did no damage to the Japanese ships. They were met with heavy anti-aircraft fire and attacked by Zeroes that had managed to launch and were patrolling overhead. Against this withering combined fire, few of the planes got close enough to launch their torpedoes. Those who did manage to fire watched in dismay as their torpedoes bounced off enemy hulls, all duds. Then they went down in flames.

Combined and concentrated enemy fire began against these planes while they were still eight miles from their targets and continued until they all were down except one. A young Navy Ensign, George H. Gay, was the only survivor. He completed his run against very heavy fire, dropped his torpedo, pulled up and skimmed the enemy carrier's deck at less than ten feet, then splashed his shot-up plane into the sea. His gunner had been killed but Gay spent the rest of the day in the sea, watching the fight. He also spent the night there, kept afloat by his life preserver and raft. The next day after having given up on rescue he spotted a beautiful Catalina, landing to recover him.

The fourteen TBDs from *Enterprise* fared only slightly better than *Hornet's* planes. Four, attacking without fighter escort, survived their torpedo runs against the Japanese ships, but scored no damaging hits.

Although at a great price, these two Devastator attacks performed a valuable service to their fellow pilots. Their costly efforts pulled down nearly all of the Zeroes to such a low altitude that the following SBDs from *Enterprise* and *Yorktown* had a much easier time of it.

These Dauntless dive-bombers came in at about 1020 while Nagumo's ships were still dodging the Devastators. The *Akagi* took two hits, which set her afire, forcing Nagumo to transfer his flag to the light cruiser *Nagara*. The *Akagi* remained afloat throughout the battle, but was in such bad shape that her captain and crew abandoned her at about 1915, ordering her sent to the bottom by a torpedo from one of the Japanese destroyers that had been providing screening cover. The *Kaga* took four direct hits that put her out of action but remained afloat all day until 1925 when she blew up and finally sank.

American flyers began breaking through the protective fire and scoring left and right. The *Soryu* took six hits, three from the air and another three from torpedoes fired by the American submarine *Nautilus,* which arrived on the battle scene at shortly after 1400. The ship's aviation gasoline storage tanks exploded and broke the ship in half and she immediately disappeared. In his book, Admiral Spruance questions these reported hits. He presents strong evidence that this ship was actually the *Kaga,* that only one torpedo struck, and it, like so many others, was a dud.

Just as Spruance had hoped and planned for, the American attacks had caught the ships in the process of refueling and rearming planes from the Midway attack. Nagumo lost three of his four carriers, but even with these vital ships and their planes gone, he was determined to fight on. The last carrier, *Hiryu*, had escaped damage by getting far out of position during some earlier action to escape the torpedo planes. Spruance: *"Defeat now stared the Japanese starkly in the face, but they felt the battle had to be continued as long as possible to reduce our future striking power."*

When *Akagi* was shot from under Nagumo, the *Japanese Striking Force* commander temporarily passed his command to Rear Admiral Hiroaki Abe on board the heavy cruiser *Tone*. His Air operations command, he gave to Rear Admiral Tamon Yamaguchi on the *Hiryu*.

At about 1050 hours, two float planes from the Japanese cruiser *Chikuma* sighted the *Yorktown* task group and alerted eighteen dive-bombers and six fighters from the *Hiryu*. The float planes then guided the twenty-four aircraft in to strike *Yorktown* at around 1200 hours. Patrolling U.S. aircraft, along with withering anti-aircraft fire from the ships knocked down or turned back most of these enemy planes, but those that got through scored three devastating hits which set fires and within twenty minutes the big carrier was dead in the water. Her crew got the ship underway again in about an hour, just in time to face a second attacking strike force from the *Hiryu* which appeared in the early afternoon. Ten Kate torpedo bombers, along with six Zero fighters, made their run and half were shot out of the sky. Four of the Kates made it through the firing and came in on their torpedo run at masthead level. They released torpedoes at about 500 yards and two scored direct hits which left the carrier not only dead in the water again, but listing so badly to port that she was abandoned just a few minutes later.

The speed with which *Yorktown's* crew had put her back in service fooled the Japanese. They believed the second attack to be against a different carrier. They had by now spotted the three U.S. carriers, but thought they had destroyed two of them. The second strike still did not completely finish the *Yorktown*. The battered ship not only stayed afloat after being abandoned, but even regained some degree of stability. Salvage crews boarded the ship next day and placed *Yorktown* under tow. One of Nagumo's floatplanes spotted her early on 5 June and directed a submarine out to finish her off. The sub found the carrier on the 6th and put two torpedoes into her belly. Early on the morning of the 7th, *Yorktown* went to the bottom.

Before the first attack, *Yorktown* had sent out ten bombers as scouts and they were still in the air after the second attack doomed their carrier. At 1445 these scouts spotted *Hiryu* along with nine smaller ships and immediately reported their location back to Spruance. At 1530 the admiral ordered a launch of twenty-four SBDs from *Enterprise*. Ten of these planes were *Yorktown* refugees, recovered by *Enterprise* after her sister carrier was attacked by the Japanese, while the others were all veterans of earlier strikes that had been refueled and rearmed. They found *Hiryu* and her screening ships at 1700. Using the same tactics that had worked in their morning attacks the dive-bombers scored four direct hits that operationally finished Nagumo's fourth and last flattop. The cost to the Americans was the loss of three SBD bombers and their crews. *Hiryu* suffered the same fate as her sister carrier *Akagi*. She floated, in flames, until at 0510 the next morning when torpedoes from one of her own screening ships sent her to the bottom.

During all this action, Admiral Yamamoto, still miles to the rear and receiving conflicting and misleading battle reports, considered himself fortunate to have drawn out the U.S. Pacific Fleet and thought he was giving them a beating. Shortly after noon, when he heard of *Hiryu's* first strike against *Yorktown,* the Japanese commander sent messages ordering the *Aleutian Screening Group* and Admiral Kondo's *Second Fleet* to join him and the *Main Body* by noon the next day, June 5. He would then, he thought, finish off all the U.S. ships and occupy a much-coveted prize, Midway.

Even after he received word of the fate of all of Nagumo's carriers, Yamamoto acted in a confused manner. A full hour and twenty minutes after he was told of the loss of the last Japanese carrier, Yamamoto sent out a message that reported to his commanders that the U.S. fleet was, *"practically destroyed and retiring to the east."* Then he called upon Nagumo, the *Invasion Force* and the *Submarine Force* to *"immediately contact and destroy the enemy."* This strange message caused one commander to remark, *"In the light of the whole situation....so strangely optimistic a message suggested to me that our Commander-in-Chief was deliberately trying to prevent the morale of our forces from totally collapsing."*

Nagumo's own morale obviously needed to be boosted to keep him in the battle. At 2130 hours he radioed Yamamoto - *"Total enemy strength is four carriers, six heavy cruisers and fifteen destroyers. They are steaming westward. We are retiring to the northwest escorting Hiryu. Our speed is eighteen knots."*

Yamamoto's response was to relieve Nagumo and replace him with Rear Admiral Kondo. Later messages from Kondo told the Japanese commander-in-chief that there was little hope of finding the U.S. Fleet until after daybreak the next day. After a sleepless night Yamamoto reversed himself, abandoned the Midway disaster, and ordered complete withdrawal.

Admiral Spruance did not know of Yamamoto's decision. After Admiral Fletcher's transfer from the doomed *Yorktown* to the *Astoria*, Spruance felt more isolated than ever. He thought a vastly more powerful surface force was somewhere nearby, possibly with additional carriers that had come in with the *Main Body* or with some other enemy force. He saw his problem as avoiding any combat in which his forces would be heavily outgunned, especially at night. At the same time, he wanted to stay within air support distance of Midway in case the Japanese should renew the attack. He succeeded in this plan but in the process he lost touch with the enemy fleet. He was not to regain contact until 6 June but the retiring Japanese fleet didn't successfully evade all U.S. forces.

In the early morning hours of 5 June, U.S. submarine *Tambor* spotted a retiring Japanese column of six ships, four cruisers and two destroyers. When the Japanese in turn sighted *Tambor*, their erratic evasive action resulted in the mid-sea collision of two cruisers, *Mogami* and *Mikuma*. The two remaining Japanese cruisers retreated at flank speed, leaving the pair of injured cruisers to lag behind with only the two destroyers to screen them. The *Mogami* with a slightly damaged bow and the more severely hurt *Mikuma* leaving a wide, slick trail of oil behind, were vulnerable but the destroyers managed to keep the U.S. submarine from gaining a favorable firing position. *Tambor* stalked them all night then reported their position at first light.

Captain Simard launched twelve B-17s from Midway to attack these ships. The Flying Fortresses had difficulty locating the targets and Simard then gave a Marine bombing squadron the job. Captain M.A. Tyler with six SBD-2s and Captain Richard E. Fleming with six SB2U-3s took off at about 0700 to attack these ships, then reported to be about 170 miles due west of the atoll. They located the ships about thirty minutes later and Tyler led his division out of the sun straight toward the stern of *Mogami*, while Fleming and the other Vindicator pilots peeled off for a direct run on *Mikumba*. Both groups met heavy anti-aircraft fire, but Tyler and his flyers bracketed their target with six near misses that managed to cause some damage topside to *Mogami*.

Captain Fleming's plane was hit and severely damaged, but he managed to stay on course and at the head of his attack formation. He then crashed his plane directly into the after gun turret of *Mikuma*. Fleming's suicide dive spread fire into the air intakes of the starboard engine room causing gas fumes to explode in the engine room, killing all hands there. This was a severely damaging blow to the cruiser, which was previously unharmed except for the light hull damage sustained earlier in the collision with *Mogami*. Both cruisers were now badly hurt, and continued their slow westward withdrawal as their prospects of escaping the Americans' avenging fury faded.

Admiral Spruance's carrier planes finally caught up with the cripples the following day, 6 June, sank *Mikuma* and inflicted so much damage on *Mogami* that it would be two years before she was able to re-enter the war.

The Battle of Midway, which many military experts and historians consider the decisive naval engagement of the Pacific War, was over. The U.S. had lost ninety-eight carrier planes and the *Yorktown*. Japanese carriers lost a total of 322 planes according to some reports. This number is suspect and exceeds the normal number of aircraft for four aircraft carriers of this era. There was no arguing, however, that the casualties were significant and the loss of the cream of her naval pilots was felt even more strongly by Japanese high command. This, along with air losses in battles over Guadalcanal, was a blow from which the Japanese never recovered.

The carrier planes had decided the larger issues of the Battle of Midway, but the actions of Marines on the atoll had also been considerable, from developing the base, through defense preparations, right to the end of the fighting. Brave Marines on the ground as well as in the air made their contribution, many sacrificing their lives.

I may not have hit any enemy planes with my .50 caliber machine gun, I'm not sure, but my water plant was partly responsible for the Japanese being caught at Midway. When I found out about that much later, I felt proud. My part of the Midway story ends this chapter and shows that a combination of strategy, foolish blunders and plain luck carried the day for us and began Japan's downward slide as a world military power.

Marine valor and sacrifice were a major factor at Midway. The 3rd and 6th Defense Battalions had both provided labor, vigilance and flak to the defense effort. The aviators and ground personnel of MAG-22, at a cost rarely approached in the history of U.S. naval aviation, faced a far superior enemy and took a heavy toll on them. At a cost of forty-nine Marine lives and fifty-three wounded, Midway had destroyed fifty-three enemy aircraft. Twenty-five dive-bombers and eighteen Zeros were shot down in their air actions and another ten went down from anti-aircraft fire.

These efforts added to those of Fletcher and Spruance's men sent the proud *Imperial Fleet* scurrying for home without firing a shot from its superior naval guns. Yamamoto took small comfort in the fact that his northern operation had secured two bases in the Aleutians. *"What good the rice bowl if the rice is gone?"* he asked.

Unlike most of his officers, Yamamoto had some appreciation of American industrial resources and military strength. He knew that destruction of the U.S. Fleet early in 1942 was vital to the year's plans for control of the Coral Sea and American sea lanes to Australia and New Zealand, and to the success or failure of Japan's entire war effort.

Now that the Japanese were soundly defeated at Midway, they could no longer downplay the setback they had received at the battle of the Coral Sea just before the disaster at Midway during Phase One of their 1942 war plans. Phase Three, occupation of the Fijis, Samoa and New Caledonia was scrapped by the Japanese high command. Admiral Spruance - *"The Japanese catastrophe at Midway definitely marked the turning of the tide in the Pacific War."*

From arrogant, overconfident offense in the Pacific war, the Japanese were soon turned to face-losing defense and then to complete defeat. U.S. plans for a first offensive already were well advanced, and the rest of 1942 was the gloomiest period in Japan's military history.

I knew nothing of any part my water plant played in the battle. When they tell me about it now, I say, "Oh yeah. It seems like I remember somebody telling me about that. Is it important?" I don't want credit for anything I did by accident or on purpose either back then and I still don't like to talk about my next stops, Guadalcanal and Tulagi. I will share a few memoires of them, but don't ask me to get too specific. I just can't do that, even to this day.

Guadalcanal and Tulagi

The Beginning of Japan's End

After the Midway attack, I spent my days much as I had during the preceding weeks, except that there was a lot of cleaning up to do. While we provided fresh water for the men, my helper and I also cleared away debris and helped put things back in order. I worked hard keeping the distillation unit in top operating condition and providing as much water as possible every day.

After about a month, I was told to get my gear ready once more, this time to report aboard a troop ship that was loading at the dock. As usual, I wasn't told where I was headed. Several of us who had been assigned to Fleet Marine Force elements were soon going to be reunited with our old units and I was glad I would finally rejoin my buddies of the 3rd Defense Battalion. I didn't know that we would actually be reinforcing and assigned under the 1st Marine Division. When I heard the name of the island we were headed for, I didn't recognize it, but I would never forget it. We were on our way to Guadalcanal.

This island was nothing like the Pacific atolls I had seen so far. It was nearly 100 miles long and twenty-five wide and the land ran from plains and foothills along the north coast to a mountain backbone that dropped straight down to the south coast. It rained all the time and the daily question wasn't if, but how long, how hard, and how deep. The temperature was always pushing ninety degrees and water was everywhere making for a very unhealthy climate. Mosquitoes thrived and loved to sink their spikes into people causing malaria, dengue, and lots of other fevers, some without names or cures. Fungus and other infections also afflicted us. Dengue Fever almost did me in and many other men in my unit also suffered with it. Dengue doesn't stay with you as long as malaria, but it can make you feel even worse. It's a viral infection, also carried by mosquitoes and causes fever and joint pain so bad that it is also known as "break-bone" fever.

Guadalcanal was bad. I'm not going into many details and you can read up on it if you want to but I don't feel comfortable talking about much of it. I'll just say it was worse than terrible and leave it at that.

Telling you that we were in such bad shape when we left that they sent us back to the States for more than a year right in the middle of the war, should be sufficient. After about three months on Guadalcanal, I was sent to a nearby island called Tulagi, which if anything was worse.

The U.S. Joint Chiefs of Staff had began revising their basic Pacific policies the day Admiral Yamamoto suffered his defeat at Midway and turned tail back toward Japan. From now on it was to be offensive planning rather than defensive. The chiefs wanted a strategy that would contain Japan, prevent her advancing toward Australia, and safeguard U.S. communications lines in the Pacific area. The idea was to put Marines in the lead on all ground assaults against the Japanese, then let the Army mop up.

Disagreement between the Army and Navy came up time and again over how to conduct the war in the Pacific. The Army thought MacArthur should lead all assaults while the Navy felt it was their show. They saw Navy ships leading the way, Marines landing to take strategic islands and the Army being used in a backup and replacement role to come in and free up the Marines and Navy for yet another advance.

Admiral Ernest J. King, Commander-in-chief of the U.S. Fleet and Chief of Naval Operations had made this clear as early as 18 February. He had told Army Chief-of-Staff General George C. Marshall that he considered it necessary to garrison certain South and Southwest Pacific islands with Army troops to free up the Marines for an island-hopping offensive against the Japanese.

Shortly after the Battle of the Coral Sea, MacArthur presented his plans for an attack against the enemy at Rabaul and requested aircraft carrier support, additional troops and more planes. Nimitz immediately rejected this plan, telling the general that the Navy's carriers were too scarce to be committed in such restricted waters as the Solomon Sea. The admiral had a plan of his own. He wanted to capture Tulagi, a smaller island close to Guadalcanal using just one Marine raider battalion.

Admiral King favored this plan at first, but on June 1, he reversed himself and sided with MacArthur and Marshall that Tulagi couldn't be taken by just one battalion. The victory at Midway had improved the U.S. position in the Pacific. On 25 June Admiral King advised Nimitz and Vice Admiral Ghormley, Commander of South Pacific Forces, to prepare for an offensive against the lower Solomons, a group of volcanic islands in the southwestern Pacific that included Guadalcanal and Tulagi, administered by Great Britain, but Japanese held, and New Guinea.

King's plan was to use Marines under CinCPac to take and occupy Santa Cruz Island, Tulagi and adjacent areas, then turn them over for Army troops from Australia to garrison. D-Day for his operation, he said, was about 1 August. The job looked impossible to Ghormley, who had just taken over his Pacific command after a hurried trip from London where he had been Special Naval Observer and Commander of U.S. Navy Forces in Europe. The First Marine Division, picked to make the Solomons landings, was in the middle of an administrative move from the United States to New Zealand and Marshall and King continued to argue over who should command what. Marshall disagreed with the Navy's claim to the right of command. The operation lay in the Southwest Pacific, he pointed out, so MacArthur should be in charge.

For his part MacArthur also felt he should take control but King wasn't about ready to begin debating geography with the Army. The forces involved would not come from MacArthur he pointed out, but from the South Pacific. King doubted that MacArthur was in any position to help anyway because the nearest land-based bomber field was nearly 900 miles from Tulagi. The question was becoming a hot potato and the Joint Chiefs decided to handle it. The last thing they wanted was the services fighting with each other over issues of command. There was already an enemy that demanded every ounce of fight the U.S. had to offer and the Joint Chiefs finally solved the conflict by issuing the *"Joint Directive for Offensive Operations in the Southwest Pacific Area Agreed upon by the United States Chiefs of Staff."* These orders set the taking of the New Britain-New Ireland-New Guinea area as the objective but broke it down into three phases aimed at resolving the dispute between MacArthur and Nimitz. Phase One would be the capture of Santa Cruz and Tulagi along with the placing of units on adjacent islands. Nimitz would command this operation, with MacArthur concentrating on enemy air and naval activity to the west. To remove the Army's geographic claim on the Phase One operation, the Chiefs shifted the boundary to place the Lower Solomons in the admiral's South Pacific area.

MacArthur would then command Phase Two, seizing the other Solomon Islands and placing men in New Guinea, and Phase Three, the capture of Rabaul and bases in New Britain and New Ireland. The Joint Chiefs would handle any questions of timing, tasking and command changes from one area to another. Phase One was given the code name "Operation Watchtower" but so many problems came up that the troops were soon calling it "Operation Shoestring."

The Navy's plans were outlined by CinCPac OpOrd 34-42. Nimitz directed Ghormley to ensure that all assault forces met at sea for a conference to allow the commanding officers to gather face-to-face and discuss operations in detail. The meeting took place at a point south of Fiji, well out of sight of land to make sure no enemy agents on the island spotted the ships as the assault forces were arriving from many directions. The 2nd Marines commanded by Colonel John M. Arthur steamed in from the north aboard the *Crescent City, President Adams, President Hayes, President Jackson,* and the *Alhena,* escorted by the carrier *Wasp* and a destroyer screening force. The regiment had been on board for nearly two months, lying at anchor in the harbor at San Diego. The 1st Raider Battalion, which had been picked up at Noumea, was aboard the four converted destroyer transports of Transport Division Twelve.

Colonel Robert H. Pepper, who had commanded the 3rd Defense at Pearl Harbor, was still in charge. Most of the 3rd had remained at Pearl since the attack. The safety of the Hawaiian Islands was still an open question and the battalion had been very busy since war's outbreak, guarding resources there. Now they embarked aboard two troop ships, *USS Betelgeuse* and *Zeilin,* headed for a linkup at sea. A carrier force, built around the *Saratoga* and *Enterprise,* was also on its way by a slightly different course.

The conference took place as planned, some 400 nautical miles south of Fiji. It opened immediately on board *Saratoga* as soon as all major commanders arrived. His Chief-of-Staff, Rear Admiral Daniel J. Callaghan and senior Communications Officer, Lieutenant Commander L. M. LeHardy, represented Ghormley, who was unable to attend. Several grave problems surfaced right away. General Vandegrift, who was to be our commander, learned he would not have adequate air and surface support for the unloading phase of the operation. Fletcher wanted to retire within two days of the initial landings. This meant that transport and supply shipping would have to clear out within a very short time. Vandegrift argued this would put his Marines in acute need of supplies from the start, but the Navy wouldn't budge. When Callaghan reported to Ghormley by message on the conference, he was skeptical of Fletcher's plans for such an early withdrawal. *"This sounds too optimistic to me,"* he wired, *"but Fletcher and his staff believe it can be done. I believe the Navy supply ships will not be fully unloaded for three or four days at best."* Ghormley too believed that the ships could not be pulled out so soon, but he made no move to override Fletcher's decision. From this event, we on Guadalcanal were to suffer greatly.

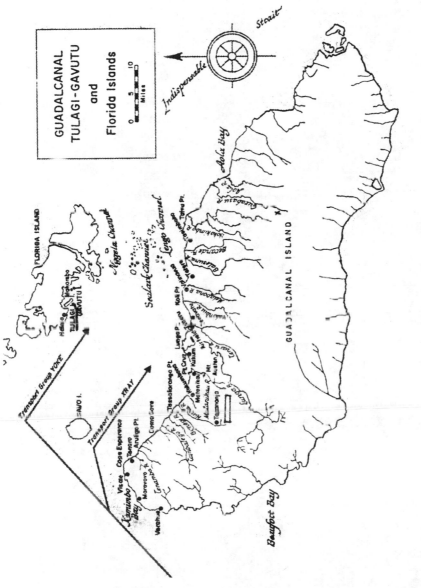

Guadalcanal and Tulagi

Guadalcanal Camp

Following the conference, the group proceeded to the island of Koro in the Fijis for landing rehearsals the last three days of July. General Vandegrift labeled them a complete waste of time and effort. He was very upset with the Navy for what he was sure was the shortchanging of his Marines on a grand scale and he was never to forgive them for it. Speaking of the practice landings several years later in 1948, he told a group at Princeton University that the operation was, *"a complete bust and waste of time and energy."*

The Navy wouldn't release their landing craft for the exercise and this made it impossible for the Marines to conduct any realistic practice landings, although some training in loading was done and the big ships were able to practice their gunfire. A still-steaming Vandegrift later wrote the Commandant of the Marine Corps that the Navy's landing craft weren't in decent operating condition, even at the practice. Twelve of them, he noted, were out of commission on one ship alone.

At nightfall on 31 July 1942, up came all anchors and the ships got underway, leaving the island of Koro behind. The carrier task force proceeded north and west while the transports and their destroyer screen steamed slowly but steadily toward the Solomons. Twenty-three troop ships, nineteen transports and four destroyer-transports carried the Marines who were numbered somewhere between 18,500 and 19,500 in Navy and Marine 1st Division records. Luck was with the convoy. Weather conditions at sea were very favorable during the last two or three days of the approach. Low clouds, strong, gusty winds and heavy rainsqualls made detection unlikely and there were no signs of enemy aircraft, submarines or other ships. Enemy patrol planes were grounded at Rabaul on 5 and 6 August because of bad weather. The convoy headed west from Fiji, well to the south of the Solomon Islands chain. Courses were gradually shifted to the northward, and the night of 6-7 August found the ships due west of the western end of Guadalcanal.

The task group, labeled Task Force 62, was commanded by Admiral Turner and divided into two main Transport Groups, one destined for Tulagi and the other for Guadalcanal. The 3rd Defense Battalion, my outfit, was split between the two groups, with *Betelgeuse* in Transport Group X-ray including a searchlight battery commanded by Captain Kirgis headed for Guadalcanal. Transport Group Yoke with *Zeilen* and the rest of the battalion headed for Tulagi. Not with either group, I was on my way from Midway on another ship and joined up with them on their first day on Guadalcanal.

At 0310 hours 7 August 1942, the entire force was steaming at twelve knots off Cape Esperance with a distance between the two groups of about six nautical miles. Transport Group X-ray was deployed in two parallel columns, one of eight ships, the other of seven, with 1,000 yards between the columns and 750 yards separating each ship from the next. The rugged mountain outline of Guadalcanal was just visible to starboard when a course shift to 040 degrees was ordered. A few minutes later the two groups separated and headed for their landing sites.

X-ray, preparing to land on Guadalcanal, shifted course still further starboard to 075 degrees, proceeding along Guadalcanal's coast. Yoke, on a heading of 058 degrees, passed to the north of the island just outside Savo Island toward Florida. Final approaches were made without incident and there was no sound until 0614 hours, when the supporting ships opened fire.

That morning was to prove something of a Pearl Harbor in reverse for the Japanese. Later study of Japanese wartime messages show the enemy was aware that U.S. forces from Hawaii were somewhere in the area. Warnings of possible attack were sent out by Japanese high command to Central Pacific outposts, but the message reached only Rabaul while points south were only told later for information purposes. Commander of the Japanese Twenty-fourth Air Flotilla, Marshall-Gilbert-Wake area, sent the message along the next morning, 7 August at 0430 but it was already too late. Less than an hour later he received a frantic return message from Tulagi that the U.S. striking force had been spotted in Sealark Channel at 0425, five minutes before the "informational message" had been received.

The landings took two days and nights. My ship arrived early on the first day and pulled right in to drop us off. I was happy to be back with my unit and my old boss, Captain Kirgis, although we were now assigned to the 1st Marine Division. Units of the 3rd Defense were there from day one until after the Japanese had all been killed or sneaked away and long after the 1st Marines were evacuated. After three months on Guadalcanal, I joined a group of men being sent to Tulagi by landing barges to reinforce the men of the 3rd Defense over there because so many of them had been killed or seriously wounded. Every day on Tulagi we killed a lot of Japanese, often standing off their famous "Banzai" suicide attacks, but every night they would land a bunch more and we would start all over again the next day. It was dangerous and tiresome work. It's important to understand the landings, because the fact that the Navy departed early left our Marines without sufficient materials to conduct the fighting in a proper manner.

On the first night of the landing, Task Groups X-Ray and Yoke separated just north of Cape Esperance at 0240 hours and X-Ray made for the transport area called "Red Beach" or "Beach Red" on Gaudalcanal in a double column at twelve knots. No enemy activity was encountered or observed and the preliminary naval bombardment of the coastal areas at 0613 aroused no response. X-Ray's ships reached their area at 0645 and immediately began to lower landing craft. Among these Marines were some selected units of the 3rd Defense Battalion, including 18th Antiaircraft Company, which I joined up with. Across the channel, Group Yoke including most of the 3rd Defense arrived off Tulagi without incident and all hands got the word from Captain Ashe that H-Hour would be at 0800 hours. The first beaches to be hit were on larger Florida Island, followed by Tulagi. General Vandegrift held up the assault on Guadalcanal's Beach Red until he received word of the successful landings on Florida and Tulagi, then he released the first wave of assault troops to move toward Guadalcanal's beaches.

Nine "spotter" aircraft were launched from cruisers, three each from *Vincennes, Astoria* and *Quincey.* Their job was to fly liaison missions between commands and to spot for the artillery. During the landings, these aircraft were used extensively marking beach approaches with smoke bombs to help guide the landing craft and also spotting targets for naval guns. Even on this point General Vandegrift showed his displeasure with the Navy brass, and he strongly disagreed with the use of such precious air resources for these routine jobs. The planes were not carrier planes but tiny amphibians, which were winched over the side of the cruisers by special cranes and then took off from the water's surface. Vandegrift's division air officer firmly agreed with his commander's concerns. The Navy held firm, Admiral Turner saying he considered it necessary to *"accurately mark the extremities of the landing beaches"* as directed by the operations order, and they proceeded to do so, while the Marine commander fumed. The little planes made eight extremely low altitude runs on the beaches, four on each extremity. Vandegrift pointed out once again that this maneuver would result in serious, if not complete loss of the planes if the beaches were at all defended. He considered this foolhardy at a time when the planes were critically needed as "eyes" to gather information about Japanese defenses and the progress of the landings.

Vandegrift got very little information from these planes, but it wasn't because of lack of trying by the pilots. Guadalcanal's heavy clouds and dense jungle cover made their work almost impossible and the tension of these first landings on hostile beaches caused some serious errors in judgement. One pilot reported siting "many enemy troops" but when questioned for more explicit information he decided that the "troops" actually could have been cows. Except for cows, another observation plane pilot reported no enemy activity around Lunga Point and the Beach Red area, even as late as 0859, a few minutes before H-Hour. Fifteen minutes later, this same pilot spotted some enemy trucks moving on the Lunga airfield several thousand yards west of the landing beach.

Meanwhile the 5th Marines crossed the line of departure and moved into their 5,000-yard-long approach to the beach. Naval gunfire lifted as landing craft neared the shore and minutes later, at 0910, the assault wave hit the beach on a 1,600-yard-wide front and immediately pushed into the sparse jungle growth beyond the shoreline. Two battalions expanded the beachhead against no opposition. A defense perimeter was hastily established some 600 yards inland, anchored on the west at the Tenaru River, on the east by the Tenavatu River and reaching south inland to a small east-west branch of the Tenaru. At 0938 hours, Regimental Headquarters came ashore followed two minutes later by heavy weapons units. Then the main body of troops landed and reinforced the perimeter. Next came artillery, which promptly bogged down. Howitzer troops later admitted they had brought too much gear ashore. Heavy trucks, called prime movers designed to haul the heavy 105mm howitzers, were late getting ashore because there were not enough ramp boats to haul them from the ships and one-ton trucks already ashore were too light to pull the heavy guns in the sandy soil. Vitally needed now were the powerful prime movers that were supposed to have come ashore at the same time as the howitzers. They were authorized, but so were many other critical supplies we would not be seeing on Guadalcanal until much later, if ever.

In typical Marine fashion, the artillerymen overcame the problem and reached their assigned positions with the help of a totally unexpected ally, a tractor. They took over heavy amphibian tractors as soon as they wallowed ashore loaded with supplies. Cargo was quickly dumped off and the tractors were put to work hauling big guns to their assigned positions. This was the beginning of an expanding role in which these tractors would prove useful beyond all former expectations. The amphibians did have one serious drawback that the artillerymen hadn't anticipated. Like tanks and all other tracked vehicles, they chewed up communications wire on the ground and this left the artillerymen without directions from headquarters. This type of damage was to plague Marine wiremen throughout the campaign. Lighter 75mm pack howitzers made it ashore without any trouble and the advance toward the main objective, the critically important airfield, began. At 1115 hours the 1st Marines passed through the temporary perimeter that the 5th Marines had established, about six hundred yards inland from Beach Red, and headed southwest. Their goal was Mount Austen, also known as the "grassy knoll." This small mountain, just over 1,500 feet, had been clearly visible from the sea and seemed like an easy first day's objective.

About halfway to the knoll, Colonel Clifton B. Cates put his regiment across the Tenaru River on a quickly placed engineer's bridge, which was supported underneath by one of the ever more useful amphibian tractors but the Marine's progress was soon slowed by the thick jungle. At 1330 hours, as Cates and his men struggled through the tangled growth, elements of the fifth Marines crossed the Tenaru at its mouth, then moved east parallel to the beach and toward the Ilu River. Neither advance encountered any enemy resistance.

Colonel Cates soon came to the realization that his Marines were not going to reach Mt. Austen that day as planned. The so-called grassy knoll, while visible from the sea, could not be seen once ashore. It commanded the Lunga area and was essential to taking and holding the airfield, but it lay much further inland than reports of former planters and sea captains had indicated. Under heavy packs, and with insufficient water and salt tablets, the Marine advance had managed to struggle only a mile toward their goal by late afternoon. General Vandegrift ordered the regiment to halt, dig in, orient themselves and establish better internal contact. This was welcome news for the tired Marines. Later medical reports said the weight of equipment was too much because of the poor physical conditions of the Marines. These men had been cooped up for long periods in steamy ship holds without proper exercise, and at the same time had also been fed short, often inferior rations. We would continue to have ration and equipment problems for the entire time we were on these islands.

The men thankfully dug a perimeter in the jungle and set up for the night. In spite of the quick pace with which this shoestring operation had been mounted and had thrown itself in the path of Japanese advances in the Solomons, the landing was a success. The lack of early opposition on the Guadalcanal side gave the operation some of the characteristics of training maneuvers, and the need for much additional training was clearly evident. Vandegrift regretted the fact that he had been unable to give his men additional preparation in New Zealand as he had hoped. This lack of training, said the general, *"resulted in a lamentable and uniform failure of all units to properly patrol their fronts and flanks."* If security on the Marines' perimeter was bad, logistics were worse. Transportation of supplies from ship to shore and then from the beaches to supply points inland soon snarled up and then ground nearly to a halt. Now it was Admiral Turner's opportunity to point a finger. He blamed the SNAFU on the Marines. He claimed they didn't understand the number of troops required for such work. He further stated the Marines failed to extend the beachhead limits far and quickly enough. He then aimed a barb directly at Vandegrift, complaining that there was a lack of control and direction over troops, especially in the beach area.

The trouble and its causes were neither as clear-cut nor as damning as Turner would have liked to make them sound. Marine planners had long foreseen a dangerous shortfall of manpower at this critical phase of the operation, but not knowing enemy strength, felt they could allot no more than 500 men from Colonel George R. Rowan's 1st Pioneer Battalion for the work on the beach. Vandegrift made it clear that he didn't want men used on working parties if it cut the strength of his fighting units to a level that might risk getting them shot to pieces.

Vital supplies piling up on the beach presented a juicy target should Japanese planes from Rabaul show up and concentrate on bombing the area. This endangered the operation much more severely than using more working parties would have done. As it turned out there were hardly enough Japanese forces ashore at this time to pose much of a threat. Command was well aware of the risk and that Japanese planes could easily threaten the whole venture on the beaches but they were also expecting to run into many Japanese forces in the thick jungle. The men of the shore parties would just have to work harder and make up the work of the men that were needed in the jungle.

Sailors pitched in to help the Marines clear the beach, but the cargo from the ships overwhelmed them and the area remained cluttered and vulnerable. Division officers grumbled that they needed at least another hundred men for each vessel discharging cargo onto the beach. These problems had been thought out and planned for in fleet exercises, but this was "Operation Shoestring" and the planners knew there would be shortages everywhere. The situation became so bad during the night of 7-8 August that the landing force requested the ships to cease unloading. There had been several air attacks during the afternoon, more were expected the next morning and exhausted workers needed more time to clear the beaches and disperse the gear so it would offer less of a target. Fortunately for the working parties on shore, air attacks concentrated mostly on the ships.

At 1100 hours, 7 August, a coastwatcher posted in the Upper Solomons passed the word across the watchers' network; *"Eighteen Jap bombers just passed over! Looks like they're headed for Guadalcanal."* This warning was relayed to Vandegrift and the Navy through Brisbane, Australia twenty-five minutes later. The bombers arrived at 1320 and immediately attacked the ships. The destroyer *Mugford* took a direct hit from a 250-pound bomb and suffered twenty casualties but it was the only ship struck in the attack. Antiaircraft fire downed two of the planes, Type 97 twin-engine bombers. Later in the afternoon at 1500, ten Aichi dive-bombers attacked but achieved no hits at all, and fire from the ships splashed two more Japanese planes. Fighters from Fletcher's carrier downed several more from each of these attacks.

General Vandegrift issued his attack orders for the following day at 2200 hours. Plans had been changed. Since Mount Austen appeared out of reach through the heavy jungle, and because he had only about 10,000 of us available in the entire Lunga area, he ordered occupation of the airfield and a defensive line along the Lunga River. Positions already established east and southeast of Red Beach would be maintained for now to protect supplies and unloading shore party operations until they were moved inside the new perimeter. We set up our tents near the airfield, which would later be named Henderson Field for Maj. Lofton Henderson, a Marine pilot killed at Midway. The Japanese understood the value of this airfield and holding it was not easy. Several air raids were sent directly against it. No sooner would the engineers make the field usable, then another raid would put it out of commission. On 12 August, the field engineers first declared the field ready for fighters and bombers. A seaplane had tested it shortly before but no fighters were yet available to try it out. Bombers did arrive, but they were Japanese. A heavy raid dropped seventeen bombs on the field, killing one engineer and wounding nine. It would be a while yet before Henderson Field would be operational, but all of this was still in the future. First we had to get to the field and occupy it.

At 0930 hours, 8 Aug., 1st Battalion, 5th Marines crossed the mouth of the Ilu River and headed cautiously westward along the beach toward the Lunga River and the airfield. They were supported by Company A, 1st Tank Battalion. At the same time the 1st Marines were moving from their night perimeter. Communications between units within this regiment were bad, but by nightfall 1ˢᵗ Battalion, commanded by Lieutenant Colonel Leonard B. Cresswell, had secured the airfield and reached the Lunga. The other two battalions slowed by the rough terrain, advanced only about 500 yards per hour and finally bivouacked for the night south of the airfield.

As they moved along the beach, 1st Battalion, 5th Marines encountered their first resistance as they crossed through an area in which the main Japanese force had been camped. A few prisoners were taken and interrogated and said the enemy had been caught unaware and was in no position to attack the superior Marine landing force. This fact was confirmed by a lack of stiff resistance anywhere. At 1430 the Marines consolidated their front, crossed the Lunga via a bridge just to the north of the airfield, and advanced more rapidly toward the Kukum River, a stream in the western part of the Lunga river delta. With Company D in the lead, this advance came upon the most recent main Japanese camp at 1500. The enemy force, much smaller than anticipated, had retreated in confusion and haste. They left behind large quantities of undamaged electrical gear, engineering materials, radio equipment, ammunition and food. Some improperly briefed Marines began to systematically destroy this material but were soon halted by their superiors. In the next few weeks, as shortages in their own gear grew more and more critical, these Marines would lose their contempt for this kind of lucky discovery.

Except for scattered token resistance from some of the fleeing Japanese troops heading west, air action was the enemy's main early effort against us. That would later change drastically when Japanese ground reinforcements arrived. At 1100 on 8 August, Coastwatcher C. J. Mason, an RAAF Pilot Officer, warned from his Bouganville hideout that a large number of Japanese planes were headed toward Guadalcanal. An hour later some forty twin-engine torpedo planes appeared over the area to attack the task force which, alerted by the warning, was maneuvering at top speed and using evasive tactics.

A direct torpedo strike sent the destroyer *Jarvis* limping southeast for the New Hebrides, but she didn't make it. Next day an enemy air attack sent *Jarvis* to the bottom. The transport *Elliot,* set afire when an enemy plane crashed into her, had to be beached then destroyed by her own ships. Survivors were taken on board the *Hunter Liggit* while antiaircraft fire and fighter planes from Admiral Noye's carriers shot down twelve Japanese planes and shore-based fire got two more. Carrier-based fighters downed still others west of the beach area. A total of seven American planes were lost in this, the first of many air and sea battles fought over the next several weeks.

These early attacks slowed Marine operations and unloading efforts but the beachhead slowly continued to expand. The Japanese, however, had no intentions of giving up their position in the Southern Solomons without a fierce fight, and early on 8 August a task force of five heavy cruisers, two light cruisers and a destroyer made ready to strike American shipping in the Sealark Channel. After meeting up at St. George's Channel near Rabaul, this force steamed south along Bouganville's East Coast until it noticed an Allied patrol plane overhead plotting its course. The ships quickly reversed course and headed back up the coast until the plane left. Turning again, they sailed between Bouganville and Choiseul northeast of the Shortlands and then set their course down "The Slot" between New Georgia and Santa Isabel, then on toward Guadalcanal. Word of this approaching force reached Admiral Turner at 1800 and shortly after that Admiral Fletcher notified him that the carrier force would be withdrawn. Turner then called Vandegrift to the flagship *McCauley* and told the general that without carrier protection the transports must leave at 0600 the next day.

Nearly a week before, on 2 August, Admiral Ghormley had known of Fletcher's intentions to remove the carriers on D-Day plus three. At 1807 on 8 August, Fletcher cited fuel shortages and plane losses that had reduced his fighter craft from ninety-nine to seventy-eight and again requested permission to withdraw. It appeared to observers that Ghormley had not fully expected this in spite of Fletcher's announcement at the Fiji rehearsals but now that Fletcher was formally making the request, Ghormley gave his reluctant approval. He later attempted to explain: *"When Fletcher, the man on the spot, informed me he had to withdraw for fuel, I approved. He knew the situation in detail: I did not. Then I directed Turner to withdraw his surface forces to prevent their destruction. I was without detailed information as to Turner's situation, but I knew that the Marines had landed and that our major problem would now become one of giving every support possible to Vandegrift."*

As soon as I joined my old outfit, I was finally given a Browning Automatic Rifle to carry. This raised my pay six dollars every month, but of course, we still weren't getting paid anything. The BAR with its bandoleer was more than twice as heavy as my 1903 Springfield rifle. We were short of everything and ammunition for the BAR was no exception so I was told not to fire it too often. This resulted in me either carrying my Springfield or the BAR or sometimes both, making a load three times as heavy as normal. I was the smallest Marine in our outfit and in the heat, hills and wet I began wondering if it was worth the six dollars or not, especially since I wasn't getting paid anyway.

We were camped around the airfield to protect it from Japanese attack but we also went out on patrol a lot and one thing that happened on these patrols is noteworthy. One night in the pitch dark a shot rang out and one of our NCOs went down, victim to a sniper's bullet. Just a very lucky shot, we thought. The next night the same thing happened to another NCO and the third night again. We figured the Japs must have been slipping in between the lines at night and targeting sergeants and corporals. Finally someone figured out the reason only NCOs were being hit. They were all issued watches with luminous dials that must have been visible for long distances at night. All the NCOs quickly turned their watches to the inside of their wrists and the mysterious sniping stopped. From then until today, I still wear my watch with the dial facing to the inside.

After about three months on Guadalcanal, some of us were chosen to leave for Tulagi, a small island nearby, to replace Marines of our outfit that had been killed or badly wounded in the heavy fighting. I spent the next four months battling Japs over there and it was pretty rough. It seemed like we would wipe out a bunch of the enemy one day and they would come back even stronger the next. This led some superstitious Marines to comment that they were just popping up out of the ground but we soon learned the real answer. At night they were sneaking in reinforcements in small boats and hauling off their wounded.

Toward the end of my time on Tulagi, our camp was located on a high hill from where we had a good view of the water. Our island was a port for several of the Navy's PT boats, big wooden speedboats that were the fleet's workhorses and could also launch torpedoes at enemy ships. It was one of these boats that evacuated General MacArthur and his family from the Philippines along with that country's president just before the fall of Bataan. We enjoyed watching their comings and goings from our vantage point high above.

After six months of hard fighting, the remaining Japanese evacuated Guadalcanal and Tulagi and were gone by 8 February. Another Major General, this one from the Army, had relieved General Vandegrift and the 1st Marine Division several weeks earlier. General A.M. Patch, Commanding General of the Americal Division, became commander of Guadalcanal on 9 December and the Marines there began to stand down and return to Australia. When Guadalcanal finally fell, 1st Marine Division was in Australia, the 2ⁿᵈ and 8ᵗʰ Marines were in New Zealand, and the 1ˢᵗ Raider Battalion and 1ˢᵗ Parachute Battalion were in New Caledonia. All these old island hands were spending their days resting up and fighting off recurring bouts of malaria and other fevers. We were still suffering on Tulagi, had been for months, and would be for another month or so until finally relieved. The 3ʳᵈ Defense was the only ground unit to stick it out for the entire Guadalcanal-Tulagi period and we looked it. We were in such bad shape that high command decided to send us back to the States for regrouping. We would need many new men and a lot of training before we were ready for battle again, this time on Saipan and Tinian more than a year later.

There had been several major offensives by the Japanese on Guadalcanal, both by land and out at sea. They knew too well what losing these islands meant to their future plans. On 20 August, the first American fighters arrived at Henderson Field and the next day the Japanese launched a major ground attack that became known as the "Battle of the Tenaru." Three days later a big naval battle took place called the "Battle of the Eastern Solomons." On 13 September, we fought off the second major attack in the "Battle of the Ridge." In addition to these big battles that wore us down, there were countless little battles and patrols and suicide rushes by Japanese soldiers who all seemed very anxious to get themselves killed, hopefully while taking a few of us with them. By the time we were relieved, most of us were very sick, both physically and mentally. It would be quite a while before we were fit to go into battle again.

More than a thousand Marine officers and men gave their lives on Guadalcanal and Tulagi. The cost was not as high as some later operations where the Japanese would demand even higher costs on shorter terms for much smaller islands. The total Marine and Army KIA was 1,598, with nearly 5,000 wounded, but there were many more that would suffer from debilitating malaria and other diseases for years to come. It got so bad toward the end of the fighting that a rule of thumb was if a Marine had a fever of less than 103 degrees he could not be put on light duty and he pulled his patrol missions. The cost for the Japanese was much higher. Their records show 13,000 soldiers were evacuated to fight another day but many more than that died on the islands. Some 14,800 were KIA while another 9,000 died of disease and wounds. It was a deep blow to their war effort.

When we were finally evacuated, we were sent back to Pearl Harbor for shipment on to the States. We were ready for some decent food and rest but more than that, we had heard we were going back stateside for training and furloughs and we were all more than ready for a little time off to get healthy and cure some of the homesickness.

Return to the States

Recuperation, New Men and Training

The months of slugging through the jungle on Guadalcanal and Tulagi had worn us down terribly. Not only were we fighting the Japanese, we also had to deal with mosquitoes, fungus, fever, standing water and short rations. Lack of sleep and poor nutrition brought on exhaustion and made us easy prey to malaria, dengue fever and some other diseases they couldn't even find names for. Finally, toward the end and with the islands mostly secured, the U.S. Army relieved the Marines. The shift of responsibility began in October of 1942 but the 3rd Defense Battalion was the last to leave and we stayed on Tulagi for several months even after the main body of Marines had departed. Finally, after all remaining enemy soldiers had escaped or been killed, we made ready in February to return to Hawaii for a short rest and much-needed medical treatment. Then it was back to the States for a well-earned thirty-day leave and a long training period for our many new replacements. But not me. Again I was to be left behind.

I had recently only partially recovered from a battle with dengue fever, which had done the job the enemy could not seem to do of putting me out of action. I was in a field hospital for more than two weeks, learning first hand why they called this disease "break-bone fever". Then I learned I was not to accompany my unit this time either. This was due again to a military technicality similar to the one that caused my outfit to leave me on Palmyra. I had still not been overseas the required eighteen months. Since this was the minimum time required for rotation back, I would be staying put for two more months. I guess I spent more time on Guadalcanal and Tulagi than any other Marine, but it sure wasn't because I wanted to.

Finally I was relieved with orders sending me back to Pearl from where I would soon return to the States for my thirty-day leave, some rest and further training. More than a year would pass before I saw another Pacific island. I would soon find myself back under my former CO again but he had been promoted and was now Major Kirgis. He immediately promoted me to corporal and wanted to make me sergeant, but before that happened I had to get back there and the return trip turned out to be quite a boat ride. A few dozen of us got orders to travel from Hawaii to the States together, and this time we were to cruise in style.

We boarded a big luxury liner, two men to a stateroom and were feeling pretty lucky and congratulating each other until we noticed guards at each end of the hall. They told us not to leave our rooms unescorted. We even went to the dining room at a different time than the other passengers. We figured it must be because we hadn't been near any females for over a year and there were quite a few good-looking women among the passengers. Ship's officers must have thought we would go crazy if we got near one. Some folks had a pretty distorted idea of servicemen, especially the Marines. We later learned that even the president's wife thought we would act like animals around the opposite sex and she wanted to isolate us from them completely until we had been "rehabilitated."

The next day I guess somebody felt a little guilty or had a change of heart because we were all invited to the dining room where a special show had been set up for us. Six pretty girls, who looked like professionals, danced the hula for us. We were the only ones in the dining room and I guess if we were ever going to go crazy or act like animals that would have been a good time for it but we acted like perfect gentlemen, much to some folks' surprise. Sometimes I just don't understand people's thinking.

A few days later the liner arrived in San Francisco without incident. My first impression of stateside wartime treatment of Marines was a negative one, due to a little run-in with the Red Cross. As I came down the gangplank I saw a big sign proclaiming, "Send a Message Home!" That's a great idea, I thought, because after I got paid I planned to take my furlough and use part of it to visit my parents. Since I didn't have money for a phone call or even know the number, I thought this would be a terrific way to contact them. I wrote a short message telling them I would see them soon. Next to the "American Red Cross" sign, I handed the lady my message and my parent's address and was surprised when she asked me for two dollars to send it. I searched all my pockets and was only able to come up with a dollar in change. We still hadn't been paid and when I was turned away from the message counter I felt really low. A little further along was another sign, which read "Send a message home - Salvation Army." I asked the man standing behind the table if a dollar would be enough to send my message. "It's not very long," I told him. *"Son, we don't charge service-men to send messages home,"* he said. After I sent it, I really felt good and I still donate to the Salvation Army every chance I get.

We boarded the train for San Diego and soon left San Francisco behind, headed south along the coast. After a few hours the train made a scheduled stop in Los Angeles. This was our first chance to let off a little steam and as sometimes happens, some of us let off a little too much. We had a couple of hours to kill so we all got off to look around. Before long somebody spotted a liquor store and decided it would be great if we all got ourselves a bottle. I still had no money but somebody lent me five dollars and we each bought a pint or fifth of whiskey. I had never felt the need to drink hard spirits in my life, but on this day it just seemed like the thing to do and I guess I went along with my buddies for a while but after a sip or two I gave my bottle away. I didn't care for hard liquor then and still don't touch the stuff.

Most everybody was nipping on a bottle for the rest of the train ride and as a result the trip got cut short. We were all still armed with our rifles, cartridge belts, and bayonets and a couple of guys started fooling around with their bayonets, just having fun, but then somebody got cut a little and some of the other passengers got scared. I think the train crew radioed ahead because before long we screeched to a halt and a bunch of MPs came aboard. *"Marines off!"* they shouted. We were herded aboard buses waiting beside the tracks and made the rest of the trip under the watchful eyes of the Military Police. When we got to San Diego, the buses pulled right up in front of the barracks. Some of the men were really drunk by this time and had a little trouble exiting the bus. A few dropped some of their gear and bayonets and even some rifles hit the deck, something the Corps frowns upon. The men fell off the buses and staggered around looking lost. I hadn't had more than a sip or two but some of them were in pretty bad shape. Then "the brass" showed up and observed the show.

Our barracks happened to be located directly across the street from base headquarters. It was the start of the workday and a group of officers were arriving, many driven by their wives. You should have seen the expressions on their faces. It seemed pretty funny to some of us at the time, the shape we were in, but one senior officer, a colonel I think, had seen more than enough. You could only allow enlisted men to get away with so much, even if they had just returned from a war. *"Get those men into the barracks and out of sight,"* he shouted to a captain, *"and keep them there until they sober up!"* The captain passed this word to the MPs who again herded us, this time into our barracks. When we got inside some of the men were still in a playful mood and one of them fired a couple of rounds through the ceiling. Before we knew it the MPs were back and took away all our ammunition and the fun was pretty much over.

It took us a few days to get our pay squared away and put in for furloughs. One day some of us were listening to the radio when Eleanor Roosevelt came on a news program. She said something like, *"I think all these Marines coming back from the Pacific should be put in special 'rehabilitation camps' until they can be taught how to reenter society and treat our young ladies properly."* It made us all pretty sore to hear that, but after the way some of us had acted recently, I figured that maybe I couldn't disagree with her too much.

In a couple of days my furlough came through and I got paid but I decided to do a little local sightseeing before I went up north to visit my parents, and wasted no time heading straight for downtown San Diego. I stopped at a little café for a cup of coffee and a pretty young lady sat right down beside me. *"Hi Marine,"* she said. She was really nice looking and had fiery red hair. She said her name was Mary and asked me what I was planning to do for fun. I told her I was thinking of going down to spend the day in Mexico because I had never been there and had nothing better to do. *"I would just love to go with you,"* she said. That sounded real good to me. This was to lead to many days and nights of pure fun with a wild and crazy redhead, just what I needed after eighteen months of island life. We walked all day and looked around in Mexican shops until she caught sight of a liquor store. *"We could sure use a couple of those,"* she said, pointing to some pints of whisky in the window. Thinking back to the problems on the train, I was sort of against this idea, but she insisted so I bought two for her. She then split a hole in the lining of her coat and slipped both bottles in and I started thinking Mary really knew what she was doing.

When we got back to the border crossing one of the Mexican guards hollered, *"Hey, what's that lump in your coat?"* He found both of Mary's pints and took them away and this made her quite angry. She accused the officer of wanting them for himself so I got her out of there in a hurry. We had a good time in Mexico and even if Mary was a little wild, I figured I deserved some fun after all I had been through so we decided to meet again. We spent several days together before I left San Diego to finally visit my parents and I saw her again when I got back. This was a brand new experience for an Alabama boy, and I enjoyed it quite a lot.

The second night my beautiful redhead told me to meet her at a certain streetcar stop. She said she had a surprise for me and she wasn't kidding. I had been waiting for only a few minutes when a streetcar pulled up. I didn't pay much attention until I heard my name called and looked up to see Mary wildly waving for me to get aboard. I could hardly believe my eyes. She was driving the thing. What next, I wondered , then jumped on and went along for a free ride until she got off work. She drove to the end of the line, dropping passengers as she went, then rolled an out-of-service sign into the little window and we were ready for the run back to the trolley barn. Her last stop was right at the top of the steepest hill in town. "'Let me drive," I begged her. "You're havin' all the fun." To my surprise she immediately changed seats with me and off we went, tearing down that hill at full speed. It was great fun and made me think back to Bill and our runaway ore car up on Red Mountain. That was the first time I had ever driven a streetcar and I haven't driven one since nor have I ever met another girl like Mary, my wild, fun loving redhead.

Mary also enjoyed going to the bars, drinking, dancing, listening to the music and waiting to see what excitement might happen. She had a favorite place that I took her to several times where I usually bought us a big pitcher of beer. Only sailors and Marines and their girlfriends went to this particular bar. The Army didn't dare come in because if they did a fight at once broke out and they got pitched right back out again. There was quite a lot of rivalry between the services back then, and not all of it was the friendly type. If the Army didn't show to stir things up, the sailors and Marines would eventually go at it among themselves and fights often broke out, with Mary enjoying every minute of the action. The little band always yelled out how they were everybody's friends and then they kept right on playing while ducking flying bottles and furniture. When glass and chairs started soaring into the air, I looked up and was amazed to see my redhead right in the midst of it, throwing with the best of them. I decided this might not be the girl I wanted to take home to meet my parents but we parted friends when I left for overseas again and I really enjoyed all our good times together.

I spent most of my furlough in Southern California then traveled up to Oregon for a week to visit my parents. I had gone up to Los Angeles some weekends but spent most of my weeknights in San Diego, either sleeping in the barracks or going out with Mary. On one weekend in LA,

I went out to Hollywood to keep a promise I had made to myself to meet a woman I had never met in person but still felt very close to. I went to try and see the "Reveille With Beverly" show. Back on Palmyra, I had nightly tried to tune in this program and enjoyed it a lot when I could find it. I wanted to meet Beverly in person, if possible, and tell her how the state-side tunes and light-hearted talk had always cheered us up over there.

Military personnel had priority for seats at the show so I pushed my way down front until I was sitting right on the first row. The music played, the curtain opened and there she was. In the middle of the show Beverly asked if anybody had a request or wanted to say anything over the air so I got up my courage and raised my hand. She called me straight up to the stage and asked me what I wanted to say. I told her that we had listened to her on the radio every chance we got overseas and that she really kept our spirits up. She got a bit emotional about that and the next thing I knew she gave me a big, wet kiss, smack on my cheek. I enjoyed that a great deal.

I met another girl while in Los Angeles. She wasn't wild like Mary but she made a deep and lasting impression on me. The day after the "Beverly" show, I left my hotel and went looking for some breakfast. A nearby café was very crowded, but there were two stools open so I took one and ordered. The other one was right next to me and as luck would have it, a very good-looking young woman soon came up. *"Is this seat taken?"* she asked. "No," I managed to say and she sat down beside me and ordered. I tried to think of something else to say but I was quite shy and it was obvious at first glance that this girl was not only a "looker" but a real lady as well. Finally, I stuttered my name out and she told me hers was Alice. When we finished eating I asked her if she wanted to go for a walk. *"Oh yes,"* she said. We walked for a while and Alice told me she worked at Fox Studios and could get tickets to shows anytime she wanted. "I like to go to shows," I told her. She said she also sang in a church choir and was on her way to sing at the morning service. *"Would you like to go?"* she asked. I would have gone anywhere with Alice and I might have been falling in love at first sight. Alice looked even more beautiful in her choir robe and thoughts of a lasting relationship and maybe even marriage were dancing in my head. Then visions of returning to the war flashed before my eyes and I decided marriage wouldn't be the best plan at this stage of the game.

A few days later I boarded a bus for Redmond, Oregon to see my parents. It was amazing to me that after having divorced when I was a little boy and marrying someone new, my parents had later decided they just couldn't live without each other. They divorced their new mates and remarried, a most unusual thing, especially back in those days, but I would have to say they lived pretty much happily after that.

The bus headed north and soon we were passing through snow banks as high as the bus windows. It was a big change from the swamps and jungle and I really welcomed it. I soon arrived at the little Army-Air Force base where my dad was stationed. He had been a private in WWI, and when war broke out again, he volunteered to come back into the Army in any capacity. Since experience was at a premium, they sent him to Officer's Candidate School and made him a lieutenant. He was already a Captain and Provost Marshall by the time I showed up. I spent a few days with my parents and I guess I enjoyed myself but it was a little awkward, us finally together again after all those years of separations. I had a real good time when my dad took me to the flight simulator building and they let me fly the trainer. It was just like being in a plane.

Then it was back to San Diego for a little more R&R, if you could call it that. The schedule I set for myself for the next couple of weeks provided for very little relaxation and almost no rest at all. I spent most weeknights with Mary the wild redhead and whenever I got weekend liberty I went up to Los Angeles to see Alice. Life was good but the schedule was wearing me out. I needed the Corps to rescue me before it was too late.

Finally, it was time to get back to work so I boarded another train for the four-day trip back to the East Coast. I arrived at Camp LeJuene, North Carolina and reported to my new commanding officer. Imagine my surprise when it turned out to be my old commander who was a major now and not surprised to see me in the least. He knew I was coming because he had asked for me and he promptly promoted me to Marine corporal. Major Kirgis said he had wanted to make me sergeant, but would have to make me corporal first and then there was a 30-day waiting period before I could become sergeant. I was happy with my promotion because a corporal was considered a noncommissioned officer and Marine NCOs were excused from many details such as KP.

Major Kirgis had brought four of us "old hands" in to be his new section leaders. We were all seasoned veterans of the Pacific war and had served under him on Guadalcanal and Tulagi. He told us we would each soon have our own section of about twenty-five men, although for the present we had none. We had lost so many senior people on the islands that promotions were coming hot and heavy and we would soon have new men. Most of them were green replacements for us to train before returning to the fighting. *"Right now while we're waiting for your men to arrive,"* Major Kirgis said, *"I want you section leaders to get as much training as possible yourselves."* I was to get plenty over the next few months.

I went to an advanced water engineering school right on Camp LeJeune. Mixed in with the schooling was some liberty and it wasn't any time at all until I found a friendly little bar in a neighboring town. I could nurse a beer for hours there while I relaxed and enjoyed the atmosphere. One night, a pretty young lady sat down beside me and introduced herself. She said her name was Judy and she was a student at a nearby all-girls college. Judy and I soon became good friends and saw each other most weekends until I had to go to another base for still more training. I looked her up when I got back and we dated some more until my men arrived and then the training became so intense that the only maneuvers were out in the field. I don't know what courses Judy was taking at college, but she was something else. After the advanced water engineering course the Major sent me to radar school, down in South Carolina. He had learned our unit was going to have a radar set when we went back overseas and he wanted me to become qualified on it.

I headed off for Fort Jackson near Colombia, South Carolina to attend a radar school, which was hosted by the Army. Here I learned radar fundamentals and also found out that some things are done a little differently in the Army than in the Corps. I picked up a lot about radar during the next few weeks but I also had one or two minor run-ins with the Army. I had hardly unpacked before the sergeant in charge of my barracks spotted me and said, *"Hey, Corporal, I'm putting you on KP right away so you can get it over with."* I thought that over for a minute before replying, "I'm sorry Sergeant, but Marine NCOs don't pull KP, and I'm an NCO." The sergeant looked at me like he couldn't believe what he was hearing. *"Oh, so you don't want to pull KP huh? Well, we'll just have to see about that, won't we?"* With that, he stomped out of the barracks. It wasn't long before he was back, with a smug look on his face. *"The Lieutenant wants to see you, buddy,"* he said. I told him in a nice way that was all right with me but Marine NCOs didn't pull Kitchen Police duty. It was starting to look like I was in for more than just radar training at this school.

The rules governing KP aren't the only differences between services. The way enlisted men report to superior officers is also special to each service branch. In the Army, a soldier remains covered, with hat on. He knocks, reports, and salutes saying, *"Private Jones reporting as ordered sir."* Marines and sailors, on the other hand, don't wear covers when reporting. We placed them under our arm and, since we don't salute unless covered, we reported in the same way, with no salute.

Knock! Knock! Knock! *"Come,"* said the young lieutenant in his most military-sounding voice. My garrison cap tucked under my arm, I marched up to the desk and said, "Corporal Abbott reporting as ordered, sir." The Lieutenant didn't even bother to glance up at first. *"Now, what's this about you not wanting to pull KP, Corporal?"* he said. Finally, he looked up, preparing to return a salute but none was there. *"Hey, Marine! Don't you salute your officers?"* he cried. "Yes sir, we do," I answered, "but not indoors. We don't wear our covers or salute indoors, except for a few special ceremonies," I told him in an informative manner.

"Oh yeah?" croaked the Lieutenant, obviously flustered, *"and is there anything else you Marines don't do?"* I looked at him for a minute before replying. "Yes sir, NCOs don't pull KP." The Lieutenant didn't like any of this, but he finally dismissed me and I turned on my heel and went back to my barracks. They didn't try to assign me any more details while I was at school, and the Lieutenant and I didn't cross paths again. The Army is slow to forget what they think might be the hint of an insult from another service and I'm positive they tried to get even with me on my last day there.

There weren't any other incidents until after I finished school. My orders specified transportation from my barracks back to home base, so I called for a ride to the gate where I was to catch the bus back to Camp LeJeune. It was more than three miles from the barracks and I had my bag to carry. I think the Lieutenant was still mad at me because his office told me to find my own way to the gate. *"You can walk, for all we care,"* said his sergeant on the phone. I then called the radar school's commanding officer, the Lieutenant's boss and told him my story, but he said there was nothing he could do to help. "Sir," I said, "Could I read you what it says here in my official orders?" I read him the part about authorized transportation, which stated that the Army had agreed to furnish me transportation to the bus station after I completed my training.

"The school's over, sir. I passed it and now I'm just trying to follow my orders and get back to my base," I said. A few minutes later a jeep pulled up at the barracks. *"Is there a Marine corporal here who needs a ride to the gate?"* asked the driver. I got in and he dropped me right at my bus. *"Boy, they were steamed over at the school when the CO called and ordered them to give you transportation on the double,"* said the driver. I think the Army was glad to see the last of me, and the feeling was mutual.

When I got back to base there were promotion notices on the board. Not only had I been made a sergeant, Major Kirgis was promoted to Lieutenant Colonel at the same time. I joked to the other section leaders that if he kept getting promoted every time I did, I would never catch up with him.

We were still leaders without any followers. I was supposed to have twenty-five men to train but so far I had none. I was sent to yet another school and this time they wanted me to learn to speak Japanese. My buddies joked that my Alabama drawl was too heavy to ever be understood by the Japanese and, as things turned out later, they were probably right. After language school, I returned to find my men waiting for me and we began an extensive training program aimed at keeping them alive in battle. During this period, we went through so many equipment changes it nearly made us dizzy. We were all issued M1 rifles and no sooner had we become proficient at firing them then they were taken away. They then gave us carbines, which the veterans fell in love with at first sight. They were light, quick, reliable and easy to fire. We began to practice with them immediately. They would be great in the jungle, we agreed. We were pretty sure that's where we were headed as soon as training was over. No sooner had these thoughts been expressed than they issued us heavy arctic gear including parkas, snow boots, long johns, the works. It looked like our next stop would be Alaska, not some Pacific island. Next day we were ordered to turn the arctic clothing back in. Now it was anybody's guess where we would be heading.

During this training phase, I was walking along the street with one of the other section leaders when we noticed a manhole cover had been removed and someone was working on the communications wiring underground. In a second a head popped up. It was a Marine all right, but she was very pretty and had blond hair. *"What the hell is that?"* asked my buddy, astonished. "That's a woman Marine," I told him. I had heard they were bringing women into the Marine Corps for some jobs, but this was the first one we had seen and it was quite a shock. It didn't take most of us long to get used to the idea, but some guys never could accept the concept. *"Women in the Corps, what's next, petticoats for us?"* they asked. Some Marines even thought up a very politically incorrect term for them, one which stuck for years. *"There goes another of those B.A.M.s,"* they would grumble. Asked what that meant, they would be more than proud to say, *"That stands for Broad-Assed Marine. Don't you know anything?"* I didn't care for the term and never used it myself but I do remember asking myself if the heavy metal cover to the hole would now have to be renamed a "person-hole cover." The term "politically correct" hadn't been dreamt up yet.

After a few months our training on the East Coast was completed and we loaded up and headed back to California. Arriving in San Diego we were sent straight out to Camp Elliot, a tent area just across from Miramar Marine Air Station. They had failed to put in any hot water for us and this was in mid-winter. We had a tough time shaving and showering in that icy water and some of the men said they were missing that arctic gear the Corps had taken back over at LeJeune.

We did some more combat training here, honing battle skills we had already practiced in North Carolina. One unhappy incident occurred about this time, which was a little too realistic and that gave us some fighting training we hadn't bargained for. It took place downtown on liberty and not on the training field. Several of the men returned from Los Angeles beat up or worse and we learned that several Latino gangs were battering and knifing Marines and Sailors. The gang members were easy to spot because they had an outlandish mode of dress. They called themselves "Zoot-Suiters" and wore loud suits with baggy pants that had tight cuffs at the bottom. A long chain dangled from belt to pocket and from the end of the chain swung a wicked-looking knife. A group of us decided to go to Los Angeles and do something about these gangs before one of us got killed. We went to town, ran into several groups of these gangsters, and took care of business, Marine fashion. We were later told that the gang problem in Los Angeles had quieted down a lot. In later years these incidents in Los Angeles and elsewhere were labeled, "The Zoot Suit Wars" and some liberal writers tried to convince readers the gangs were just a bunch of innocent boys having fun. These writers weren't the ones attacked, the gangs weren't at all innocent, and it was definitely no fun.

A couple of weeks after the Zoot Suit occurrence, we boarded troop ships and put to sea, again headed for we knew not where. I would have to say we were pretty much combat ready by this time. We by-passed

Hawaii and finally anchored in a lagoon near the small island of Eniwetok. This atoll, along with another called Bikini, would become well known and controversial after the war because of nuclear tests performed there. We waited several days for a convoy and when it showed up, we were on our way again. We landed this time on the island of Saipan where I spent the next three months before moving a short distance over to smaller Tinian Island to remain for the final year of the war. The story of my fifteen months on these two islands is told in the next chapter and it was on Tinian where I happened to lead the last patrol before the end of the war.

Saipan and Tinian

Smith vs. Smith
The End for Japan and the Last Shots Fired

In May of 1944, we boarded a ship headed for what turned out to be our last island battles, on Saipan and Tinian. After about two months of fighting on Saipan, I was sent over to Tinian to continue combat there. It was from Tinian that the B-29 bomber took off to drop an atomic bomb on Japan and speed the end of the war. There were two bombs dropped a few days apart. That was a very different kind of fighting compared to what we were doing on the ground but both contributed to ending the conflict. During the final days of hostilities, I was camped next to the Army and was present when Colonel Tibbets told reporters, officials and troops about dropping his bomb from the Enola Gay onto Hiroshima. He said he felt this would mark the end of the war, but that's getting a little ahead of my story.

At the Washington Planning Conference in February and March of 1944, one thing was plain; the need to have a base from which aircraft could reach The Philippines, Formosa and the China mainland. Those present felt that from such a base they could interrupt most Japanese lines of supply and communications. The new base must also allow for an airfield that would permit U.S. heavy bombers to reach and attack the Japanese homeland. It was extremely important, planners agreed, to bring the war home to the Japanese as soon as possible as this was the sure way to end the conflict.

Our troop ship rested at anchor in a deeply sheltered cove with water that was deep, warm and inviting. The island seemed to have no elevation, only endless coconut trees stretching as far as I could see, even from the ship's highest lookout points. Sounds of shouting, laughter and loud splashes came continually from the shore side of the ship where Marines were indulging in a little "horseplay" while enjoying the water to the fullest and letting off the steam of restless anxiety. We were anchored just off Eniwetok Atoll, 9 June 1944 waiting to join a convoy for a major assault, and everyone knew it. The few who were aware of the name of our objective weren't talking. Loose lips not only sink ships, they also sabotage amphibious assaults. Many of the Marines jumping and diving

Mack Abbott and Marines on their way to Saipan

Landing at Saipan

into the warm lagoon didn't know the name of the nearby island, let alone where we would be landing. The name wouldn't have meant anything to us even if someone had come up and whispered it in our ears. It was a place called Saipan.

We had a good time swimming and spent most of our days in the water. We leaped from the deck, sometimes diving, sometimes "cannonballing," swim for a while, then climb up the rope ladder, lay in the sun for a few minutes, and do it all over again. We stayed at anchor for nearly a week, enjoying ourselves, but pretty soon we ran low on water. Most ships can't make much fresh water unless they are at sea and soon we were bathing and shaving in briny, itchy seawater and nobody liked that very much. Finally we weighed anchor and joined a lot of other ships in a big convoy headed for parts which were, at least to us, unknown.

Early on the morning of 15 June 1944, Marine landing barges loaded with troops, amphibious tanks and tractors hit the southern shore of Saipan Island. It was scheduled to be a joint Army-Marine assault and next day, elements of the Army's 27th Infantry Division landed to join the battle. Situated some 1,300 miles from Tokyo, Saipan was ideal for American purposes. The Japanese were well aware of the island's strategic importance and were prepared to take us on and fight to the death for it. They focused their full attention on and committed mountains of resources to the battle for Saipan and Tinian. After our successful landing on Saipan however, Radio Tokyo made what was for Japan a drastic announcement. The war in the Pacific, they admitted, had reached, *"a very serious stage."*

The offensive on Saipan gave the Americans trouble from the first day. Four days of "softening-up bombing" prior to the landings had almost no effect on Japanese troops and gun emplacements. Years spent digging in had left both guns and men nearly unreachable. Natural and man-made caves and depressions provided Japanese troops with countless ready hideouts and firing positions. Their mortars and artillery disabled many of our amphibious craft before they even made it ashore.

In spite of the heavy fire, some 20,000 Marines were on the beaches by the end of the first day. They dug in as best they could near the shore and prepared to repel a massive Japanese counterattack expected that first night. Both sides suffered heavy casualties and bloody scenes played over and over day after day. The taking and holding of Saipan and Tinian proved to be extremely costly to the Marines. The Army also sustained heavy losses on Saipan, although they never made it over to Tinian.

The two regiments of Army Infantry landed the next day and joined the 2nd and 4th Marine divisions for a push inland. Eight days of heavy fighting followed. Marine Lt. Gen. Holland M. "Howlin' Mad" Smith, Commander of the Fleet Marine Force in the Pacific was designated overall commander of the ground forces. On the 23rd he announced his intention to kick off an island-wide coordinated thrust to the north.

The 4th Marine Division took the right flank and the 2nd took the left. The Army's 27th Inf. Div. Regiment was assigned the center of the push. While the Marines on both flanks attacked in their normal highly aggressive manner, another General Smith, Army Major General Ralph Smith moved his soldiers much more deliberately, hoping in this way to keep his casualties to a minimum. These tactics caused the center of the attack to drag, sag and finally to collapse inward, leaving the Marines isolated. Both Army and the Navy brass were about to learn why the overall commander was nicknamed "Howlin' Mad." One Marine general was more than a little "ticked off" by these events.

On June 24, when the 27th Inf. Div. again ground to a standstill, "Howlin' Mad" had seen enough. He went directly to the commander of the U.S. Fifth Fleet, Admiral Raymond Spruance, the man charged with overall responsibility for the operation. He demanded that the Army general be relieved and Spruance agreed. With Army General Smith gone and a new commander in place, the Army finally began to keep pace with the Marines. Twelve days later, two of the main objectives, Garapan and the seaplane base at Tanapag Harbor were taken. The cost to the Americans was high. Nearly 3,500 were killed, 1,374 in the first two weeks and the wounded totaled 13,400, more than half of these in the first 14 days. Nearly 1,000 missing men were never accounted for, but the island was taken.

On 8 July 1944, Lieutenant General Yoshitsugu Saito, commander of Saipan's Japanese defenders arose early. His batman had cleaned the general's uniform and person as much as possible after 23 days of intense fighting. The battle for Saipan was all but over and Saito had decided it was time for him to depart. He dined fastidiously on canned crab, downed a generous amount of sake, walked to a flat rock, sat down and began to address his men. His speech went in part: *"I advance alone to seek out the enemy, follow me."* With these words Saito plunged his short Samurai sword deep into his own innards.

When death seemed too slow and the possibility of showing pain became a reality, Saito's adjutant, as instructed beforehand, put a pistol to the back of his general's head and fired one shot. Marine General H.M. Smith declared Saipan secured the next day.

We had all the trouble we could handle with the Japanese soldiers on Saipan and Tinian but there were also Japanese civilians to contend with. They often acted like they hated and feared us more than the soldiers did. We found out later that the Japanese propaganda people had been telling the civilians what barbarians the Americans were, especially we Marines. I guess if I had been told that someone would eat my baby while committing unspeakable acts upon me, I might have been terrified too. When I rode into the beach at Tinian on an LST after spending two months on Saipan, I saw several Japanese bodies floating in the surf. I found out later that these were civilians who had committed suicide rather than be taken by the American "barbarians."

The civilians on these islands had emigrated from Japan after they came under Japanese control at the end of World War I. Many had been colonists for nearly thirty years and considered the islands their homes. The civilian men joined Japanese soldiers to defend what they thought of as their homeland and some of the women also had a few tricks literally up their sleeves. Several Marines lost their lives before we learned to be very cautious of surrendering civilians. A favorite trick of the women was to surrender to a group of Marines, get close, and then quickly lob a hidden hand grenade into the midst of their would-be captors. We lost quite a few men to this trick before the word got out.

A lot of our time on Tinian was spent trying to root the Japanese out of caves and tunnels. They had spent many years constructing these defenses and they were very effective. Sometimes when our patrols took a cave system we found a little underground city. Once in a while we would either take a cave or find it unoccupied and there would be some Japanese goodies left inside. One day I led a patrol up to the mouth of a cave and peered cautiously into the gloomy interior. I could hardly believe our good luck when I spotted a nearly full case of sake just sitting there. The Japanese always seemed to have a good supply of this potent fermented rice liquor but they usually took much better care of it than this. It looked too good to be true and one thing I had already learned was that when something left by the Japanese looked this good there was usually literally a string attached. A favorite trick of the enemy was to leave a knife, gun, sword or other great war souvenir connected by a nearly invisible line to a deadly charge of explosives. If in a hurry, they would just tie the booty to the pin of a grenade. Many Marines picked up what they thought was a grand war momento left behind by some careless enemy soldier only to be blown to smithereens. It seemed unlikely that they would waste nearly a full case of sake to kill a few Marines but we decided to take no chances and inspected it carefully.

It took us some time to make sure the sake wasn't booby-trapped, then we carefully checked each bottle to make sure it wasn't poisoned. Everything turned out OK and all we could figure was that we had caught somebody on moving day and boy, were they going to be upset when they came back. We took it all back with us and had a great time toasting the thoughtful enemy we had stolen it from. We couldn't believe our luck but, as they say back in Alabama, even a blind hog will root up an acorn once in a while. Our luck didn't hold for very long though, because somehow the word got out that we had found a treasure. All of a sudden we were the most popular men on the island and discovered we had good friends we had never even met before and that put a quick end to our celebration. Oh well, what the heck, we figured, the fortunes of war and all that.

Sometimes we were witnesses to just how brutal the Japanese could be. One day while on Tinian I got a call on the field phone. *"Hey Mack, we got a report that a guy from a unit close to yours got captured by some Japs and he's in a cave not far from you. Check it out, will 'ya?"* I took a dozen men and headed for the location given me. When we got there we discovered the Japs had already left. We then found the man deep in the cave, right where I had been told he would be. He was dead and had been mutilated and castrated. I could respect the Japs as soldiers and sailors but I didn't have much use for them as human beings. Bestial behavior is not necessary, even in war.

After we secured most of the fighting on Tinian I had some time on my hands again. I still liked aircraft, even though my hopes of learning to fly had been dashed by the Japanese attack on Pearl Harbor. Rather than hang around camp, I often made my way down to the airstrip, beg a ride with any plane going out on a mission that was willing to take me, and off I went. They could often use someone to man a machine gun because they were usually short-handed. We flew over Japanese-held islands and fired at trucks, planes, gun emplacements and other targets. I logged a lot of hours like that and towards the end got pretty good at aerial gunnery.

I also drove my jeep down to our Tinian headquarters at the other end of the island nearly every day. This was quite a distance and a sort of release from routine for me. I saw many interesting things on these trips.

Except for stragglers and holdouts in the caves, most of the Japanese were dead or gone by this time and life on Tinian was changing. One day as I drove along the beach coming back from HQ, I noticed quite a number of Marines standing out in the water. I couldn't figure out why they were doing that so I stopped to have a closer look. Suddenly one man took hold of another and gave him a good dunking beneath the surf. Was this a new kind of game? Then I noticed that the man who was doing the dunking had crosses on his collar. He was a chaplain, a Marine minister, and the men were being baptized. Religious feeling goes way up in wartime. I know mine did. Some men forget their religion as soon as they are safe again but I never did. I still attend church regularly and thank God every day for protecting me during those war years.

On another occasion coming back from HQ, I decided to take my jeep on a little sightseeing ride. As I rounded a curve I ran straight into a Seabee's camp. I had already met some of these men in the past and I knew a little about them. They were civilian workers whose outfits were called "Construction Battalions," and that's where their name came from, Seabee for C.B. I also knew they liked Marines a lot because we were the guys out there keeping the Japs from visiting them late at night. The most important thing I had learned from past experience was that Seabees usually ate very well. It was just about lunchtime so I decided to stop by and say hello. *"Come on Marine,"* one guy yelled when he saw me, *"you guys are always welcome around here!"* I sat down with some of the men and told them where our camp was. "We could sure use a shower set-up over there," I added. A couple of days later a truckload of Seabees showed up and, in no time at all, we had a fine shower. After they installed the shower, I invited them to a lunch of Marine rations. They were good sports about it and grinned and joined us.

During lunch one of the Seabees told us how upset they all were about what they had seen at a movie theatre just before they had shipped out to Tinian. *"It wasn't the movie that bothered us,"* one Seabee said, *"but the news clip afterwards. I was with the 50th Seabees when they built the airstrip on Midway Island. After we finished, the Army Engineers came in and relieved us. In the news clip it told all about what a fine job the Army had done building the airstrip. That was one long, hot and dirty job and not even a tiny mention of the Seabees. Oh well, what can you expect? The Army makes all of those military news films anyway."* One of my men looked up from his rations. *"Yeah,"* he added, *"I've seen some of those news films too. The way they tell it, the Army is winning this war single-handedly, with*

MacArthur leading the charge. It makes you wonder what the rest of us are out here for. "I didn't say anything but I thought to myself that it wasn't the Army or the Seabees either that had been taking the brunt of the Japanese attacks in the Pacific. It was the Marines but we never felt the need to be singled out for recognition. We just did our jobs and covered each other's backs.

Marines will look for anything to keep themselves entertained on those rare occasions when they are not busy working or fighting. On Tinian there were a lot of small, bony range cattle roaming around loose. After the island was pretty well secured and we were making mostly routine patrols, we would sometimes catch a couple of these cows browsing in what was left of some old sugar cane field. We hooked them to two old farmer's wagons we had found and had a great time racing each other. One day one of the men decided he would play rodeo cowboy and ride one bareback. Before he landed he had already learned a valuable lesson. There's a big difference between straddling the back of some fat, sleek horse and bumping along on the bony backbone of an old scrub cow. It was a long time before that Marine was able to walk his patrols in the proper military manner again.

Early during our months on Tinian, it was back to Marine business as usual. All the other section leaders and I led patrols almost every day. Usually our orders were to kill every enemy soldier we could and clean them all out of the caves, but sometimes we were told to try and capture a few to bring back as prisoners for interrogation. One day while leading a patrol, we were working our way down toward a group of enemy soldiers. We were on our bellies, worming our way in as close as possible. I was in the lead and just as I parted some heavy grass and peered through to see how close we were, there was an angry buzzing right at the base of the big grass clump. Several bees or wasps boiled out of the ground and began stinging me on my face and neck. I was too close to the enemy to move much and I had to just lay there and quietly take it since bee stings were preferable to Jap bullets. Fortunately, it wasn't a big nest and the bees soon ran out of venom-filled barbs. I was in terrible pain and reached slowly into my pocket for a plug of chewing tobacco I kept there for just such an emergency. I didn't normally chew the stuff, but many of us carried a plug for insect bites and stings and I chewed up a big, wet wad of the stuff and put it on my face and neck, which were burning like fire. Immediately the pain subsided and I was able to signal my men to close up on me.

Japanese POW Camp

Capt. Sakae Oba surrenders sword to Lt. Col. Kirgis on Saipan

We were so close that the enemy couldn't bring their weapons to bear and we took all six without a shot being fired. The only casualty of that engagement was my swollen face.

Not long after that action, I was ordered to bring my searchlight into operation. We pointed it out to sea so that B-29 bombers returning after dark could have a beacon light to follow into the landing field. The Japanese wanted to put our light out of action in the worst way and sent patrols against us nearly every time we turned it on. We stood them off and kept our searchlight in action. We found out later that General Spaatz had given us a letter of commendation because of all the heat we took to keep that light going and guiding the bombers in safely. We were finally relieved from searchlight duty and I was directed to move my camp and men down close to the docks where we were reassigned to the Marine 5th Division. We were next to a big, new Army camp and they were coming in to take over the "mopping up" operations. I had my men set up our camp real close to the Army because I heard they had really great chow. We had been eating poor rations since we came ashore and I didn't want my men getting all run down again, like we had at Tulagi and Guadalcanal. I hoped the Army might share a little, and they did.

Next morning after moving, I spotted a big troop ship unloading and thought it must be our Marine replacements, which we were in great need of by then. I jumped into my jeep and rushed down to the shore. Just as I got there a landing barge ran in and dropped its load. It was the Army, with fixed bayonets and blood in their eyes. *"Hey Marine, where are the Japs?"* one officer asked me. "They're straight up that road in front of you, sir," I told him. They formed up and took off at double-time and, just like I had promised they soon encountered a whole bunch of enemy soldiers. Of course, they were all behind barbed wire and had been prisoners since the Marines had brought them in.

The next day I received word from Saipan that Colonel Kirgis was asking for me to come back over to Saipan to help train the new men he had just got in. This took a couple of weeks and then I went back to Tinian once again and rejoined my section, this time with some welcome replacements. We took it easy for a couple of days and then Colonel Kirgis, who had become overall commander for both Islands when General Smith left, sent me a message ordering me to, *"Get over here, Abbott. The Japanese on Saipan are going to formally surrender tomorrow and I want you to be with me when I accept it."* I did what the Colonel ordered and caught a hop on a plane that was taking off from Tinian to land later on Saipan.

18 Jy 1945

No objection to
declassification
by AFSWP
[signature] CC

WAR DEPARTMENT
OFFICE OF THE CHIEF OF STAFF
WASHINGTON 25, D.C.

25 July 1945

1 DEC 1945

TO: General Carl Spaatz
Commanding General
United States Army Strategic Air Forces

1. The 509 Composite Group, 20th Air Force will deliver its first special bomb as soon as weather will permit visual bombing after about 3 August 1945 on one of the targets: Hiroshima, Kokura, Niigata and Nagasaki. To carry military and civilian scientific personnel from the War Department to observe and record the effects of the explosion of the bomb, additional aircraft will accompany the airplane carrying the bomb. The observing planes will stay several miles distant from the point of impact of the bomb.

2. Additional bombs will be delivered on the above targets as soon as made ready by the project staff. Further instructions will be issued concerning targets other than those listed above.

3. Dissemination of any and all information concerning the use of the weapon against Japan is reserved to the Secretary of War and the President of the United States. No communiques on the subject or releases of information will be issued by commanders in the field without specific prior authority. Any news stories will be sent to the War Department for special clearance.

4. The foregoing directive is issued to you by direction and with the approval of the Secretary of War and of the Chief of Staff, USA. It is desired that you personally deliver one copy of this directive to General MacArthur and one copy to Admiral Nimitz for their information.

THOS. T. HANDY
General, G.S.C.
Acting Chief of Staff

DEGRADED
ORDER SEC A:
BY TAG
8 F 321

151

The next day we went to the appointed spot and there was a little ceremony where the new Japanese commander bowed from the waist and presented his sword to Colonel Kirgis, The former Japanese commander having already committed suicide. *"Go back and tell your men about this,"* Kirgis told me. *"They all helped make it happen."*

A few days later, I got another call from Colonel Kirgis. He wanted me to take some men out and try to capture some Japs alive so that they could be told their commander on Saipan had surrendered both islands. Most of the enemy soldiers were hiding deep in their caves, and it was late in the day before we finally found some. We topped a rise and spotted six Japanese soldiers sitting around the mouth of a big cave. They were just talking and taking it easy. "Hold your fire." I told my men, then worked my way down close to them. I stuck my head up from behind a big rock and called out in my best Language School Japanese, "Please put down your weapons. You are surrounded by many U.S. Marines. Surrender peaceably and you will be well fed and cared for." Either they didn't believe me or didn't understand my

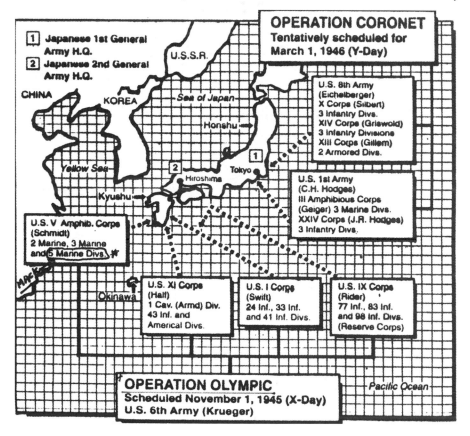

Japanese because one of them grabbed his rifle and opened up on me. I shot him and he dropped into a hole and was quickly followed by the others. I signaled my men to back off and we withdrew without firing another shot. Digging Japanese troops out of caves alive was next to impossible and I led my men back to camp and left them to go call Col. Kirgis.

On my way to make my call, I noticed quite a large group gathering around a platform and headed over to see what all the excitement was about. I recognized General Spaatz with an air officer I didn't recognize. *"Men, this is Col. Tibbetts who has just returned from a very important mission that I've asked him to tell you about,"* said Spaatz. Tibbetts then told us how he had just returned from a very secret mission to Japan, flying his B-29 bomber the "Enola Gay." He told us he had dropped an atomic bomb on Hiroshima. None of us had ever heard of an atomic bomb and one Soldier asked, *"What does that mean sir?"* Tibbetts looked at him for a minute, then smiled before he answered. *"It means the war should be over in a matter of days with no invasion of Japan,"* he said.

Later, when I called Colonel Kirgis to tell him about the patrol, I also told him what I had just heard. "We'll try for prisoners again tomorrow," I informed him. *"No, you and your men stay close to camp until we find out more about this,"* he ordered. "Yes, Sir!" I replied. Now this was an order that I would gladly follow.

Next morning as I was walking over to the shower near our camp, I heard a jeep coming up the road behind me. Things were quite relaxed and informal around camp and I was hiking along the side of the road naked as a jaybird. I heard a shriek and turned to have a look. The jeep had two Army officers in the front. In the back were two more Army officers, only these two were very flustered nurses. Well, what was I to do? I just turned my back on them and continued walking casually toward the shower. I looked when I got safely to the shower and the jeep was headed back in the direction it had come from. I guess the nurses had seen enough, and probably more than they had bargained for.

We didn't really grasp the significance of Col. Tibbets' "special bomb," at the time but we figured it meant we wouldn't have to invade mainland Japan, something we all dreaded. We knew too well the ferocity of the Japanese suicide charge and how much worse it would be once every Japanese soldier and citizen, man, woman and child, were protecting their homeland and their emperor.

Operation Downfall, code named Operation Olympic, was a Top Secret plan for the invasion of Japan that had already been finalized in early 1945. The Army, Navy and Marines were to land on Japan on Nov. 1, 1945 with fourteen combat divisions of Soldiers and Marines. President Truman had approved the invasion to begin on or about Nov 1 and the 5th Marine Div. that I was assigned to was scheduled to land on the main island of Kyushu. There would be at least 3,000 ships in the invasion and the plan estimated that in the early stages of the invasion 1,000 Americans would be killed and over 250,000 total casualties at a rate of more than 1,000 per hour would be suffered. Many experts believe that dropping the atomic bomb saved millions of lives, Japanese as well as American. I personally agree and I'm very thankful we didn't have to make that landing.

It was amazing how well the secret of the bomb was kept. General Smith, who had already left the islands says in his book "Coral and Brass" that he didn't know a thing about the bombs until he read about them in the newspapers after they were dropped. I was living right next to the guys who were loading them and I never heard a whisper about it. I knew there was "something" in a special Quonset hut at the end of the runway and a pit with a heavy-duty loading device, but that's all. One thing that both General Smith and I agree on, and I want to clear this up, is the misconception that the atomic bomb "won the war." It may have saved lives and speeded things to their conclusion but the war had already been won by troops on the ground, in the air and at sea.

It was just a few days after the dropping of the atomic bombs at Hiroshima and Nagasaki that we got the message to pack up. World War II was over at last and soon a ship picked us up and took us back to San Diego where I got my discharge.

Many of us who fought at Pearl Harbor were dismayed a few years ago when documents were released from the archives in Great Britain following what had been known as the fifty-year official silence. The documents indicated that Churchill might have lured Roosevelt into World War II by keeping secrets. He knew, according to these documents, all about Pearl Harbor. He knew exactly when and where the Japanese were going to attack and he withheld this information from Roosevelt hoping a Japanese attack would draw the United States into a global war including Europe.

The British had secretly broken the Germans "JN-25" code and this is how Churchill learned of the Japanese plans. He desperately needed the United States in the war on his side in Europe so he withheld the information from Roosevelt. While to most Americans this was a betrayal of our trust, Churchill rationalized that he needed the United States' help at all costs, and it was a terrible cost. He had also learned of the Japanese plans for Midway, but there was no way for him to tell Roosevelt that he knew about Midway without revealing that he had also known about Pearl Harbor as well, so he remained silent and took his betrayal to the grave.

 After the war Colonel Kirgis was promoted to General and I was glad to hear about that. He was a fine officer and I had served under him for practically the entire war. I was to keep in contact with him over the years and would see him one more time before he passed on. We met in Hawaii again in 1991, at the "Pearl Harbor Survivor's" reunion. It was about this time that I decided to dedicate the rest of my life to sharing the "Pearl Harbor" story with as many people as I can for as long as I'm able, especially the school kids. That's what I'm doing now at eighty years of age. We must always keep the message of "Remember Pearl Harbor" alive. If we begin to take our wonderful country and way of life for granted, we will surely lose it. There are too many people out there more than willing to take it away from us.

Military issued and carried through the whole war

Never to Be Forgotten

Survivors Reunion, the Monument, and the Association

After returning Stateside I made my way to Houston, where my parents had moved and I hoped to find a job. They were still living in a motel when I arrived so I got a room near theirs and started looking for employment, something that wasn't very easy to find even though I searched every day. There were just too many returning vets competing for too few jobs, many of which were being filled by women who were trained and already doing a good job. *"Do you have a college education? No? I'm sorry but we can't use you at this time."* The story was the same everywhere I went. I bit my tongue and didn't tell them that I didn't even have a high school diploma and I had been too busy fighting a war to even think about college.

I was soon staying with my parents in a very small house they had found. I went job-hunting every day but my future prospects weren't looking too great. Finally a friend told me that all I had to do in order to get into college was take a test so I decided that would be the smart thing for me. It seemed like every decent job required a degree so I went to the University of Houston and told them I wanted to start right away. *"You have to take a pre-test first,"* said the lady, *"and I will also need to see your high school diploma."* I thought about that for a few minutes and decided I would have to tell a little white lie. "My education records got lost in the war, but I know I'll do good on the test," I told her. It wasn't a very big lie, I told myself, because I had taken all those correspondence courses even though any opportunity to get my high school diploma had eluded me on the islands.

I started school with a little help from the G.I. Bill and soon found a part-time job at a big department store warehouse. I uncrated refrigerators, washing machines and other appliances, and prepared them for home delivery. In the course of my work, I called a girl named Janie at the main store several times. She was a home economics expert who made demonstrations for the store, which was called Foleys and we often discussed the appliances before delivery. One day I found myself downtown near the store so I decided to stop in and meet Janie. I liked what I saw, asked her if she would like to go to dinner and a movie when she got off work and she said, yes. We dated several times, soon fell in love, and after about six months, got married. About a year later our first son Carl was born and I soon discovered that supporting a family was very expensive so I once again dropped out of school to work full time. A year later our daughter Pam was born and a year after that, Paul, our younger son arrived. It was fairly obvious I wouldn't be going back to college any time soon. Janie and I worked hard to raise three fine children into adulthood. We talked often about how very proud of them we were. Since my wife passed away, my children and grandchildren have gone out of their ways to keep me company and make me happy and I appreciate them all very much.

Lft. to Rt.: Mack Abbott, Carl Moore, General Mundy and George Gaff at a reception at the Marine barracks on our 50th Anniversary at Pearl Harbor

I returned to Pearl Harbor for the big 50th reunion in 1991 and again in December 2001 for the 60th. I carried copies of this book to Hawaii with me then to share with my friends and comrades at the reunion. We had a great reunion in 1991 and another in 2001. Fifty years had passed before I returned to the place where the first shots of World War II had been fired to attend the Pearl Harbor Survivors Association big 50th anniversary reunion. The Marine Corps had set up several events to honor us for our actions during the attack and later on. There was a big parade, a reunion dinner and several other grand affairs.

When we first landed in Hawaii, I was amazed to see that the little civilian airport where I was going to take flying lessons those many years ago was now a huge international facility and most of the travelers appeared to be Japanese. The hotel I stayed at was very close to our old Marine barracks and there were about forty men from my old outfit staying there with me. It was interesting to see guys in their seventies who I had known back in 1941 when most of us were still in our teens. Some had brought their wives along but Janie was in quite poor health by this time and I didn't want to subject her to such a long trip.

It was not a one-day affair. We were entertained for several days. On the first morning we were picked up by military buses and taken to the base mess hall for breakfast. That meal sure brought back the memories for us. Then we went to the Marine air base where young, sharp, active-duty Marines demonstrated the latest weapons including landing barges, helicopters and even a field hospital. It was very impressive.

On the third day at lunch General Kirgis was sitting directly across the table from me and during the meal he called out in a loud voice. *"Abbott!"* Everybody in the vicinity looked around to hear what the General had to say. *"I know that you fired the first and last shot in World War II, at least as far as the Marine Corps is concerned, but it don't mean a damned thing in the end."* Everybody within earshot got a good laugh out of that and I had to agree with the General. That night after supper we went outside where bleachers had been erected on the parade field for another ceremony. A four-star Marine general got up to speak last, General Mundy, Commandant of the Marine Corps. He told us that our group of Marines had seen more action than any other units in the history of the Marine Corps. If it hadn't been for the Marines in World War II, our history would have turned out much differently, he said. I was thinking about that when I heard a voice behind me mutter, *"Hell General, tell us something we don't already know."* I didn't hear anybody else making comments, but I believe a lot of us were thinking similar thoughts. It had been rough duty but we had done the job and that was that. A Marine bugler then put his horn to his lips and Taps echoed across the field in honor of all the Marines who hadn't made it back. It was sad, but also quite beautiful.

Next we all made our way to the other end of the parade field where the base commander's quarters were. His back yard was all lit up and there was a fine spread of food and drinks prepared. Several of us were talking when General Mundy walked up and shook hands with each of us. He told us what a pleasure it was to meet us and how proud he was of what we had done for our country. He also told us we had set an example for all time for the Marine Corps to live up to. Now that made us all feel real good.

On December 7th there was a big parade through downtown Honolulu. A huge crowd lined the streets and it was obvious that the people of Hawaii will never forget Pearl Harbor or the men and women who were in uniform there that long-ago Sunday morning. President Bush made the trip from Washington to help us remember the day. The president had just finished contending with a war of his own in the Middle East where our military, led by Generals "Stormin' Norman" Schwartzkoph and Colin Powell, had liberated Kuwait and sent the Iraqis back to Baghdad in retreat. He gave a fine speech to the big crowd after which wreaths were laid for the deceased veterans with me laying one on behalf of Georgia's Pearl Harbor Survivors. George Bush was a naval aviator and his was a very meaningful speech.

One day soon after I returned home, I got a phone call from a reporter who wanted to interview me. I invited him out to the house and we sat down in my office to talk. He later wrote a nice article about me in the Atlanta Journal-Constitution. One of his questions really made me stop and think. *"What, if anything did you learn from your war experiences?"* he asked. I told him I had learned to pray during the war, had done a lot of it, and still do. I gave thanks every time I survived close calls or tight scrapes, and I often think of those times when I am in church now. There was a famous saying during World War II. *"There are no atheists in foxholes."* I think that's pretty near the truth.

When the article appeared, I really started getting the calls and I would have to say that the AJC and all the papers and TV stations have been very good to me and the Pearl Harbor Survivor's Association. I have more speaking engagements now than I can handle and I often ride in parades and attend numerous ceremonies. I also get up in the air once in a while, although I never did learn to fly. Recently, the Experimental Aircraft Association invited me to speak and afterwards gave me a ride in one of the strangest craft I had ever seen. The engines pointed backwards and I wasn't too sure about things until we were airborne. It was the smoothest and most comfortable airplane ride I could imagine.

General Kirgis and Janie are both gone now, as are many of those who attended that reunion more than ten years ago. I'm still here and I

Georgia Chapter Pearl Harbor Survivors Association's Memorial

keep very busy. Since that first article in the paper there have been many more interviews for the papers and TV and I spend a great deal of time speaking to schoolchildren, civic groups and veterans' organizations about Pearl Harbor and World War II. I find this work very fulfilling and plan to continue as long as I'm able.

I am also kept very busy writing letters, taking phone calls and helping with the Georgia Chapter of the Pearl Harbor Survivors Association. I'm becoming more involved every day with another association, the Sons and Daughters of P.H. Survivors and I plan to do a lot more to help promote that organization. I think it's wonderful that the younger generations want to be involved.

Every spring I visit the monument and place engraved bricks for veterans who have passed away during the preceding year. Then I return again each Sunday before Memorial Day to observe the annual ceremony where I usually arrange to have a military honor guard present. My family members always try their best to be present too and this makes me especially proud. Many of the World War II veterans need some assistance to attend but they still try to come if at all possible. I believe we must always be peace seekers, but we must also maintain these ceremonies and traditions, and remain vigilant and always faithful. I firmly believe that the fact that our country is made up of people of all races, creeds, colors and national origins is what makes this the greatest country in the world. Semper Fidelis!

"Thank you, Mr. Abbott. That was an inspiring and fascinating story. We will all be looking for your speaking dates around the country and we all wish you success on your book. We also think you should take those flying lessons as soon as possible."

"Mr. Abbott! Mr. Abbott! Wake Up! You fell asleep right here in your chair and it's almost dark." I woke with a start and looked around. Jim, the cemetery supervisor, was shaking me awake. Where were all the people? Had it all been a dream? Oh, well, I'd really enjoyed the experience, even if I did daydream it. I got in my car and headed home. I hadn't beat the rush hour but it was so late in the day traffic was dying down. I felt really well rested and ready to get on with things. After all, Memorial Day was fast approaching, plus I had several speaking engagements to make and, oh yes, I must be sure and call the airport first thing in the morning and inquire about those flying lessons.

For more information about the Associations, speaking engagements and future books, please contact:

Mack Abbott
1968 Beechwood Blvd., S.W.
Gainesville, GA 30504

www.firstandlastshot.com

Index

Symbols

1st Defense Battalion 70, 82
3rd Defense Battalion 93, 95, 112, 125
3rd Defense Battalion 39, 41, 43, 44, 45, 69, 79, 95, 109, 115, 117
4th Defense Battalion 81, 82, 83, 85

A

Akagi 99, 101, 103, 104
America First Movement 54
Anders, A.F., USN 58, 60
Arizona, USS 8, 9, 71, 72, 73, 76
Astoria, USS 106, 117

B

Bellows AAF Field 79
Bowe, Riddick 37, 38

C

Cates, Colonel Clifton 119
Chaumont, U.S.S 43, 69
Chennault, Claire 55
China Incident 54
Churchill, W. 76, 154, 155
Civilian Conservation Corps 73

D

no entries

E

Eads, E., USN 3, 7
Eastern Island 95, 101
Elliot, USS 122
Eniwetok 138, 139
Enterprise USS 83, 98, 102, 103, 105, 112

Lindbergh, Charles A. 54
Liscome Bay 75
Lunga River 121, 122

M

MacArthur, General D. 110, 111, 124, 148
Marco Polo Bridge 53, 54
Marshall, General George C. 110, 111
McCauley 123
Midway Island 6, 44, 45, 69, 83, 85, 87, 91, 93, 94, 96, 97, 98, 99, 100, 102, 104, 106, 107, 109, 110, 115, 121, 146, 155
Mikuma 106, 107
Miller, MM1 D. 73, 74, 75
Miller, Zell USMC 30
Mogami 106, 107
Monaghan 79
Mount Austen 119, 121
Mugford 121

N

Nagumo, Vice Admiral Chuichi 99, 101, 102, 103, 104, 105
Nanking Incident 57, 62
Neches 83
Nimitz, Admiral C. W. 91, 94, 95, 97, 98, 110, 111

O

Oklahoma, USS 72

P

Palmyra 6, 70, 85, 87, 91, 93, 97, 127, 132
Panay, U.S.S 53, 54, 57, 58, 59, 60, 61, 63
Patch, MajGen A.M. 124
Pearl Harbor Survivors Association 9, 158, 162
Pennsylvania, USS 75
Pepper, Colonel Robert H. 112
Pickett, Colonel Harry K. 87

Q

no entries

Vandegrift, General 112, 115, 117, 119, 120, 121, 124

W

Wake Island 80, 81, 82, 84, 85
Ward, USS 79
West Virginia, USS 71, 72, 74

X

no entries

Y

Yamamoto, Admiral 63, 75, 97, 105,108, 110
Yarnell, Admiral H.E. 54, 60
Yorktown, USS 98, 100, 102, 103, 104, 105, 106, 107

Z

no entries